C000200743

PEAKS AND TROUGHS

PEAKS AND TROUGHS

THE UP AND DOWN EXPERIENCES OF A VETERAN TREKKER

JOHN WALTON

Copyright © 2021 John Walton

The moral right of the author has been asserted.

Apart from any fair dealing for the purposes of research or private study,
or criticism or review, as permitted under the Copyright, Designs and Patents
Act 1988, this publication may only be reproduced, stored or transmitted, in
any form or by any means, with the prior permission in writing of the
publishers, or in the case of reprographic reproduction in accordance with
the terms of licences issued by the Copyright Licensing Agency. Enquiries
concerning reproduction outside those terms should be sent to the publishers.

Matador
9 Priory Business Park,
Wistow Road, Kibworth Beauchamp,
Leicestershire. LE8 0RX
Tel: 0116 279 2299
Email: books@troubador.co.uk
Web: www.troubador.co.uk/matador
Twitter: @matadorbooks

ISBN 978 180046 472 8

British Library Cataloguing in Publication Data.
A catalogue record for this book is available from the British Library.

Printed and bound in the UK by TJ Books Ltd, Padstow, Cornwall
Typeset in 11pt Adobe Garamond Pro by Troubador Publishing Ltd, Leicester, UK

Matador is an imprint of Troubador Publishing Ltd

This book is dedicated to

Angela

Who has supported me all the way

IN MEMORY OF

—

George Lowe
(Everest '53 & patron of King's Himalayan Club)

Noel Walsh
(Classic Nepal)

Frank Loveder Hon OV
(King's School staff – Everest '93 & '96, Annapurna '94)

Grant Strover OV
(Everest '96)

Scott Rennie OV
(Makalu '01)

Rod Meere
(Parents' trek Langtang '97)

Nancy Doyle
(Parents' trek Langtang '97)

Gill Spilsbury Hon OV
(King's School staff & Langtang '97)

Roger Blackburn
(Parents' treks Kangchenjunga '01 & Tibet '07)

Kirsten Smith-Cooper OV
(Share the Vision – Iceland '15)

Chris Johnson
(K2 North '12 & Kangchenjunga '18)

CONTENTS

FOREWORD
REBECCA STEPHENS MBE

I don't suppose that any of the climbers on the 1953 Everest expedition gave a moment's thought to the effects they might have down the line, how their inspiration, and actions, would ripple through the generations and still be very much alive and kicking today. But that, they are. Edmund Hillary was, and remains, a heroic figure in Nepal not so much for his first ascent of Everest with Sherpa Tensing Norgay but for his tireless work in supporting the Sherpa community through the Himalayan Trust. The leader Colonel John Hunt went on to be founding director of the Duke of Edinburgh Award Scheme, which has enriched the lives of millions of young people around the world, and wrote a couple of books that adorn many a bookshelf, including mine: *The Ascent of Everest* and an autobiography, *Life Is Meeting*.

Life Is Meeting. In these three words is described the most joyous part of the human condition: connection. It was forty years on from that first ascent, in 1993, that I had opportunity to climb Everest myself, and then, and now, almost another thirty years on, the greatest and most enduring privilege bestowed upon me as a result of that climb was meeting people who otherwise I would never have met. One such meeting was with George Lowe, the "other Kiwi" on the 1953 Everest expedition and then chairman of the UK chapter of the Himalayan Trust. I was sat next to him at a dinner, and, as coffee was served and speeches made, he wrote something on a scrap of paper and slipped it under my plate. On it, the words, "Would you like to be a trustee of the Himalayan Trust?"

Some things don't require even a nanosecond's consideration and this was one of them. I had only been able to climb Everest because of two Sherpas, Ang Passang and Kami Tchering; without them I never would have mustered the courage. Entirely selfishly, trusteeship of the Himalayan Trust would afford me the excuse to keep in touch with the Sherpas, with the Himalayas and with Nepal. And the relationship, I told myself, would be mutual. There was clearly a need for the Trust, and its ethos – to help the Sherpas and the mountain people of Nepal to help themselves – was one with which I felt wholly aligned.

As it transpired, John Walton, author of this wonderful book, had also been commandeered by George Lowe, and had been a trustee of the Himalayan Trust since 1992. Naturally enough we met at a trustees' meeting, and have enjoyed such meetings – and fundraising lectures, and walks – for over a quarter of a century. Now that is a frightening thought! It was a very long time ago now that John invited me to lecture at King's School, Worcester, where he taught. I know how much work goes into organising and marketing these events, and the theatre that night was full. It was clear that John was held in high regard by staff, pupils and parents too – everyone in the King's community.

John has a huge presence, and an even huger laugh, endearing him to children and adults alike. His charisma has drawn hundreds of people to travel with him, often to the Himalayas to raise awareness and funds for the Himalayan Trust. In the ten years since John retired from teaching, he has continued to work tirelessly to raise funds for the Himalayan Trust UK and through his efforts has added an impressive £150,000 to the funds. Few will forget that in 2015 Nepal was struck by a devastating earthquake. John was instrumental in galvanising appeals and raising money for the rebuilding of schools and health clinics.

Pupils, parents and friends of King's Worcester who have travelled with John have invariably been treated to hugely enjoyable trips, sometimes life-changing. In the chapters of this book, John recounts these adventures to far-flung places. The fun times are amusingly told; even the unpredictable and worrisome are treated with a light touch. It is an informative, charming and completely compulsive read.

Of those lucky enough to have met John at school, through the Trust, or on treks, to know of his generosity and to call him a friend, few will be surprised that he has chosen to donate the profits from the sale of this book to the two charities closest to his heart, the Himalayan Trust UK and the King's Worcester Bursary Fund.

Rebecca Stephens

PREFACE

While doing my homework before an interview to be headmaster of the King's School in Worcester in 1997, I was intrigued by the many references to the school's Himalayan Club. I had never come across such a concept in a day school. It clearly involved not only adventurous trips with associated practice expeditions but also a programme of regular events and a significant element of charitable work. Whoever was in charge of this, I thought, must be someone with rare energy and experience, and with particular skills in leadership and organisation. It was, of course, John Walton. One year into my new post, John had invited me to join his sixth-form trip to Nepal in 2000. It was an astute move to get his new boss onside in this way. John is no fool! This whole enterprise might have looked a bit risky and extravagant from the outside. The two training events I attended (a bitterly cold camp in Wales, and a section of a John o'Groats to Land's End relay walk) left me in no doubt that I was going to be severely challenged, that I was going to have the experience of a lifetime but also that I would be in very safe hands. John's sound judgement under pressure is a notable strength. He has an adventurous spirit, but assesses all risks very carefully. Nepal 2000 was, even for me in my forties, a life-changing experience. A pair of waterproof trousers that I bought for that trip subsequently went with younger members of my family, as they reached the sixth form, on trips with John to

Tibet, Ladakh and the mountains of eastern Turkey. There you have, in one family, a set of extraordinary experiences and memories that have been replicated in hundreds and hundreds of other families over twenty-six years. John has shared his passion with so many people. In the process, he has not only given them unforgettable experiences and raised their cultural awareness but also mobilised them, their families and friends to support numerous charitable projects, usually implemented by those who joined his adventures, across the globe. As fellow trustees of HTUK, John and I have made regular trips in recent years to Nepal to support education and health in the remote north-east of the country. I continue to find him an inspirational as well as entertaining travelling companion. I commend this book as an extraordinary account, warts and all, of the joys and hazards of leading adventurous trips. It is also an insight into the character of a man who is bold, competitive, big-hearted, irrepressible, sensitive, generous and hardwired to put the needs of others before his own.

Tim Keyes

INTRODUCTION

When I embarked upon these adventures in 1993, I never thought they would last as long as they have. With almost one hundred treks and expeditions completed, I look back on that first Himalayan trek and realise what a test it was. So many things went wrong and, had I not already planned a trip three months later, which ran very smoothly, I probably would not have pursued things further.

We were beset with problems right from the start. On our first night in Kathmandu, we visited a restaurant in Thamel, which was a forty-minute walk from the Blue Star Hotel, where we were staying. After the meal, the boys asked if they could take bicycle rickshaws back to the hotel. I agreed, but issued a warning about being careful and sensible. Unfortunately, the temptation was too great, and, as soon as they were out of sight, they began to race, offering encouragement to the rickshaw driver with promises of extra tips. The drivers entered into the spirit of things and started to take shortcuts in order to get one over on their rivals. Street lighting in Kathmandu in 1993 was non-existent, away from the main thoroughfares. According to one of the boys who witnessed the event, one of the rickshaws ploughed into a pile of sand in the road, bringing it to an instant stop. While the rickshaw stopped, the boys didn't, and they went careering over the head of the driver, one ending up in the sand while the other went head first into an oncoming tuk-tuk!

By the time I reached the hotel with my other adult colleagues, I was met with the news that one of the boys had lost seven pints of blood. Indeed, the boy had lost some blood from a small cut on his head but I soon realised that seven pints was a bit of an exaggeration. While the doctor considered what to do, I took out some superglue from the first aid kit and glued the two sides of the cut together.

Needless to say, no lasting harm came to the seventeen-year-olds and they all had something interesting to write in their diaries.

Something that happened on our second day in Kathmandu, while it did not manifest itself immediately, had a much more devastating effect on us throughout most the rest of our time in Nepal.

We visited a restaurant for lunch. Being aware of the hygiene risks involved, we erred on the side of caution and ordered pizza fungi. When the food came, there was a lettuce leaf on each plate, despite us not ordering any salad. The lettuce was wet and some of the moisture had spread across the plate and under the pizza. We did not eat the lettuce, knowing that it had probably not been washed in clean water. It turned out it hadn't!

Two days later, one by one, we began to feel ill. By this time we had flown up to Lukla, walked to Phakding and, when gastric trouble struck, it was the day we were climbing Namche Hill, 1000m of steep, relentless ascent. I was sick in Monjo and was later stricken with diarrhoea while climbing the hill. I wasn't alone, and stumbled over one boy in the bushes as I dived for cover!

By the time we reached Namche Bazaar at 3500m, most of the group had succumbed to sickness and diarrhoea, lying in tents in various stages of discomfort.

In the middle of the night, the doctor took five boys back down the hill, believing that they were suffering from altitude sickness. My colleague, Frank, set off in pursuit. Three returned, but two were taken back to Kathmandu and put on a flight back to the UK.

We slowly made our way up to Khunde, with our porters' loads of medical kit for the hospital. While there, I asked Liz Harding, the incumbent Kiwi doctor, if she would give us the once-over. We all had giardia!

As our trek doctor had returned to Kathmandu with two of the group, I asked Liz if there was any chance of her joining us on the trek; I had promised the parents that we would have a doctor with us throughout. Thankfully, she agreed, dropping everything and leaving her nurse, Di, in charge at the hospital.

Nearly everybody in the group was debilitated, lacking in energy and stamina. There was no way that we were going to be able to fulfil our itinerary ambitions. We could only, realistically, manage to walk for half a day. As a result we revised our itinerary, missing out the Gokyo Valley and just concentrating on getting to the top of Kala Pathar.

It was cold. By the time we reached Gorak Shep, the last camp before the ascent, the temperature was as low as -25°C. As we climbed Kala Pathar I stopped at the side of the track for a pee. As I fished around inside my various layers, I said to a passing member of the group, "My seven-year-old son has a bigger willy than me!"

"Your seven-year-old son has a bigger willy than all of us put together," was the reply.

We did reach the top of Kala Pathar, but we did not get a view. Again the trek jinx had played its part. Every day we had experienced perfectly clear, crisp, cold weather days, but on this particular day the cloud had descended, obliterating our view of Everest! Subsequently, the clear blue skies returned, for our trek back down the Khumbu.

The giardia continued to wreak havoc. Some days were better than others, but, just as you thought you might be recovering, one was struck down again. White-water rafting on the Trisuli River was worrisome at times because we were trapped on a raft.

After twenty-six days I finally experienced the three Fs: Fear Free Farting! Just in time for going home. By the time I got home I had lost 20kg! Frank, my colleague, had a couple of T-shirts embroidered in Kathmandu. The shirts were purple with a silk picture of the Everest we never saw. Written on the back was, "Been there, seen it, and this is the T-shit!" It wasn't until we were wearing them in school on our first day back that we noticed the spelling mistake. How apt.

CHAPTER 1

—

KATHMANDU CHESS SETS

I love Kathmandu. It is a vibrant, chaotic mess but is a super place to start a Himalayan adventure. After a few days you cannot wait to leave, to get into the fresh mountain air away from the noise, fumes and dirt that makes up the city. Equally, it is a great place to finish your adventure, to relax with a beer or two and to enjoy the banter you can have with bar staff and street hawkers.

I have learnt over the years not to show any interest in what the street hawkers are trying to sell. But, when I first went to Kathmandu, I was wet behind the ears and was wide-eyed and interested.

I was in Durbar Square, the square of ancient Hindu temples, and a haunt for many a street seller. I was approached by one selling miniature chess sets. In order to appreciate the chess set I had to look closely. That proved fatal. I was hooked and he was not going to let me get away.

Hoping that a quick purchase might let me focus on sightseeing, I asked, "How much?"

"Oh, I give you very good price, sir. Morning price," he replied, tilting his head from side to side as he spoke.

"Yes, but how much is good price?" I asked.

"Forty pounds, sir."

"Forty pounds? You are joking! I'm not interested," I said, as I waved him away in order to continue with my sightseeing. I rushed to catch up with the rest of the group, not wishing, at this stage in my Kathmandu history, to get lost.

No sooner had I caught up with the group than a voice came at me from behind my right shoulder. "OK, sir, £30. Is very good price. Best price."

Without looking at him, I brushed him away. I hoped that my brusque attitude towards him might make him realise I wasn't interested. But no, he stuck to me like a limpet, gradually bringing the price down.

Eventually he dropped the British pound and started asking me for rupees. By the time he had dropped the price down to less than £10, it was better for him to be paid in his own currency.

He was beginning to really annoy me now. I wasn't able to enjoy the sightseeing and I was missing out on information our guide was giving us. Funnily enough, the guide saw no reason to intervene. This street hawker was only doing his job and it was not up to the guide to prevent him from trying to make a living.

In the end, I had had enough. I turned to the man, still holding out his chess set and said angrily, "If I give you NRs200 for the chess set, will you fuck off?"

"Two hundred rupees I easy fuck off!" he said with a smile, taking all the anger out of the situation. I handed him NRs200, he handed me a chess set and he fucked off, happy at having made a sale. In the end I had spent about £1.60. Bit of a price drop from £40!

On another occasion, I decided I wanted to buy several chess sets. After several trips to Kathmandu, I knew that there was a great deal to be made by buying items and taking them back to the UK to sell, with a significant markup, at fundraising events. The proceeds would either go towards funding the next trip or support one of the charitable projects we were involved with.

On this particular occasion, I was walking through Thamel, the tourist hotspot in Kathmandu, the area where all the tourist shops, trekking agencies, bars, restaurants and hotels are. I saw a street hawker standing on a corner selling chess sets.

This time I approached him and asked, "How much?"

"Five hundred rupees, sir."

"What if I wanted to buy fifty? How much then?" I enquired.

A look of suspicion crossed his face.

"Fifty?" he said slowly.

"Yes," I said, "Five-oh, fifty."

"You need to see my boss. I take you," he responded enthusiastically.

"Where is your boss?" I asked, now beginning to feel a little suspicious myself.

"I take you," he insisted, grabbing my arm and waving to the taxi driver waiting nearby.

He bundled me into the back of the taxi. I immediately shuffled across the seat and climbed out of the other door.

"Where you go?" he asked, surprised by my actions.

"I don't trust you. Where is your boss?"

I was prepared to walk away, but he grabbed my arm and, looking up into my face, said, "It OK. Boss in store near Durbar Square. You come," he said, and bundled me back into the car, making sure he got in quickly before I could get out again.

The taxi slowly plied its way through the crowded streets of Thamel, squeezing between motorcyclists, rickshaws and pedestrians. How there was never any contact with them remains a mystery every time I am driven around Kathmandu.

Eventually, we arrived at the edge of Durbar Square to the point the taxi could go no further. We climbed out and my new friend took my elbow and guided me through the square, brushing off anybody thinking of trying to sell me something.

We left the square by the school and entered into a warren of really narrow streets and passageways. Dodging through a low arch, much more difficult for me than him, we entered a small courtyard. The brick floor was grubby. On all four sides the houses rose four storeys. There were many intricately carved window frames with shutters as there was no glass in the windows. Sharp, staccato conversations could be heard on all levels and the conversations all blended in to one.

In the middle of the far side of the courtyard there was a low door. I was guided in and ordered to follow. There was very little light, but I knew I was climbing a very steep, narrow staircase, with a low, equally steep, ceiling above it. He led me to the top floor and into a darkened room. I suddenly felt I was a prisoner. Nobody knew where I was and, if I were to disappear, nobody would know where to begin to look for me.

I was ushered to sit on what appeared, in the gloom, to be a bed. He then opened the shutters and light flooded in to reveal hundreds of chess sets stacked up against the wall.

"Wow! What a lot of chess sets," I said, unable to think of anything better to say.

"You want drink?" he asked.

Fearing I was not sure what I might get, I said, "No thanks. How much if I buy fifty sets?" I asked, wanting to get the deal done and be gone.

"How much you want to pay?" he asked, putting onus on me to make the first move.

Pausing for effect, I eventually said, "Two hundred."

A smile spread across his face. "They cost more than that to make," he implored. "We have to make some profit. Four hundred and fifty."

Another pause while I gave the impression I was thinking. "Two hundred and fifty."

"I need phone boss," he said, introducing his own delaying tactics.

"Where is your boss?" I asked. "You said he would be here."

"He no here. Wait, I speak with him." Whereupon he left me alone with hundreds of chess sets. I could hear one side of the conversation as his voice travelled freely around the building. At one point his voice rose and I feared we might not, after all this, get a deal.

Returning a few minutes later, he lowered his price to NRs400.

I responded with, "Three hundred."

He came back with, "Three hundred and fifty."

"Deal," I said, stretching my hand out to shake his.

A handshake was not enough for him, as he leaned towards me and gave me a hug. I suppose it's not every day that you sell fifty chess sets.

While I counted out NRs17,500, he gathered together fifty chess sets. Before he would accept any money from me, we had to check the quality of each set to make sure there were no broken pieces or pieces missing. This took another twenty minutes.

With all the sets checked and placed carefully into three large plastic carrier bags, I was able to give him his money, which he deftly counted between fast-moving fingers.

While descending the dark stairs, I failed to duck sufficiently and scratched my head deeply on a protruding nail. I immediately felt a stream of blood trickling over my forehead, between my left eye and the bridge of my nose. By the time I reached the muted daylight of the courtyard, I was a mess. Fortunately, I had some tissues with me and was able to hold one against the cut in the hope that it would stem the flow.

I was again led across Durbar Square, but this time people gave me a wide berth and stared at my blood-spattered face.

We picked up a taxi at New Road and requested it take us to the Marshyangdi Hotel, in Thamel. Again the journey was slow and at one point nothing seemed to be moving. Taxis had become stuck in the narrow street, while rickshaws, motorcycles and bicycles filled up every space between, ensuring that nothing could move in any direction. A policeman came to sort it out but, realising the hopelessness of the situation, wandered off and let everybody sort it out for themselves. Throughout all this I sat in the back of the taxi, holding another tissue to my head. The journey was so slow, I was either going to bleed to death or it was going to stop as the blood around the cut went crusty. Fortunately, the latter seemed to be happening, but still my head and face was a bloody mess.

Eventually, we extricated ourselves from the jam and, by taking some backstreets, began to make progress towards the hotel. That is, until we hit another vehicle. Nothing major happened but it led to an argument between drivers, adding more time to our journey. We were not too far from the hotel so my friend told me to get out and we fled the scene, with the taxi driver now shouting at us for his fare. He wasn't having a good day.

Just before we reached the hotel my chess set seller suddenly stopped, turned to face me and pushed me into the wall of a building. *What's going on?* I thought. Bringing his face up close to mine, he said, "My boss no trust you!"

"Excuse me?" I said, taken aback.

"My boss no trust you. But I do." With that, he delved into his pocket and produced a little bag of chess pieces. "You have these. They spare. In case." With that, he thrust the little bag into my pocket and the three bags of chess sets into my hands, and disappeared.

What a bizarre experience. It was a good investment. Having bought the sets for just £2.20 each, I was able to sell them in school for £7.50 each, giving me a good return for charity.

CHAPTER 2

—

PAKISTAN TRANSIT

It was January 1994 and we were returning home from the first Himalayan Club trip to Nepal. It had been a difficult introduction to the Himalayas as most of us had suffered from giardia, a debilitating gut condition that slowed us down considerably.

That was all now behind us and we were on our way home. The journey necessitated us spending a night in a transit hotel in Karachi prior to taking an early morning internal flight to Islamabad before continuing our homeward journey.

Everything was going relatively smoothly until we arrived in Islamabad. Having landed, a decrepit bus took us to the domestic terminal and baggage collection. It was really nothing more than a tin hut with a rickety old carousel that eventually regurgitated our twenty-nine bags. Loading the bags onto numerous trollies, we headed for the exit. As we did so the noise level increased dramatically. We emerged into a concourse that was to funnel us into the international terminal. All along one side was a barrier holding back hundreds of people shouting, creating a cacophony of incomprehensible sound. The noise was deafening. The whole scene was reminiscent of a 1940s black and white disaster movie where everybody was trying to escape.

As I look back on the occasion, I can see no colour; everything was monochrome.

The concourse gradually funnelled to some double doors but there was so much congestion that we were not getting very far very fast. People kept pushing in and barging their trollies into us. Eventually I organised our trollies in an arc across the whole concourse so that nobody could get through. We began to make progress.

On reaching the dishevelled official standing behind a desk just inside the doors, he ordered, "Passport!" He was clearly having a bad morning. The tunic of his uniform was unbuttoned, his tie loosened and his shirt bore sweat stains. Beads of sweat hung on his forehead and upper lip.

I explained that we were a group, that we were all together.

"Passport!" he barked.

I handed mine over.

"How many bags?"

"Twenty-nine. We are a group," I replied. His face visibly dropped. At this point somebody leaned over me and handed his passport to the confused official. He wandered off. Would I ever see my passport again?

Eventually, he came back, hovered, hesitated, gave the queue barger his passport back before turning to me and asking once more, "How many bags?"

Twenty-nine," I repeated.

"OK. I count bags. Go!"

The first trolley eased past him. "One, two, three, four. Next... five, six, seven, eight. Next... nine, ten..."

"Those are not our bags," I interrupted as somebody else pushed in with their trolley.

"Back, back, back," he commanded, letting the interloper through. "One, two etc. etc."

We got a little further this time before another rogue trolley broke our lines, utterly confusing the poor man.

"Back, back!" he shouted getting more exasperated. Unfortunately, he seemed to be getting more exasperated with us, who were doing nothing wrong, rather than those who were pushing in.

After a third failed attempt, he thrust my passport into my hand and shouted, waving his arms giving direction, "Go! Go!"

We did not get very far as the queue now led us to the X-ray machine. Although we tried to remain together, it was less important here, so long as the twenty-nine bags that we put on came off the other end.

Having negotiated the X-ray machine, we had to manoeuvre our way through a queue for check-in. As I had all the tickets, I suggested that the group gather in a corner with their hand luggage while I managed the check-in process. There was still a lot of noise and people barging their way in, but gradually I made my way towards the front of the queue.

Standing in front of me was a Pakistani man in a bright red velvet jacket. His jacket was the only colour that registered with me that morning. I kept thinking how out of place it was.

As we neared the front of the queue he turned to me and said, "What a fuckin' dump this is."

I was so taken aback by the cockney accent and what he said, I replied, "Pardon?"

"What a fuckin' dump this is," he repeated.

"Oh, have you been here on holiday?" I asked, at a loss as to what else to say.

"Nah, sold a car to a mate. Come over 'ere from Walfamstow wiv the paperwork. Taken me free fuckin' weeks! What a fuckin' dump. Can't wait to get back to Walfamstow for pizza and chips."

With that he was called to the desk and the conversation finished as quickly as it had started.

Check-in went quite smoothly. Returning to the group, I handed out their boarding cards prior to making our way through yet more security to the departure lounge. This was a bland room with colourless seating and a very sticky floor. Of course, the only palatable drink on offer was orange juice, but it would appear from the state of the floor that most of it was spilt rather than drunk.

Fortunately, we did not have to wait long as the process of transferring from the domestic terminal to the departure lounge of the international terminal had taken nearly four hours.

Ironically, when our flight was called, we lined up opposite the gate in an orderly manner, while other passengers pushed in from the sides. It was we, however, who got told off for not queuing properly and for pushing in!

While it was a very traumatic experience passing through Islamabad Airport, having survived it, I felt it had enriched my life's experience. I would be following the same route in three months' time and, now that I had done the transfer, I was looking forward to sharing the experience with a second group. Amazingly, it was not to be. Gone were the crowds. Gone was the noise. There wasn't even a Pakistani car salesman from Walthamstow! We sailed through in a little over half an hour and had to spend the rest of the wait sticking to the floor in the departure lounge.

CHAPTER 3

—

TOO MUCH SNOW

In early November 1995 there was a huge snowfall in the Everest region. It was triggered by a cyclone in the Bay of Bengal, causing at least two metres to fall over a relatively short time. That amount of snowfall triggered avalanches, one of which had devastating effects on a campsite at Pangka in the Gokyo Valley. During the night of 12 November a wall of snow came cascading down the slope, completely engulfing a trekkers' camp, burying it and killing thirteen Japanese trekkers and eleven Nepalese guides and porters.

Out of this tragic event came a remarkable story of survival. A porter, with his arms and legs encased in solid snow, fortunately found his head in an air pocket partly created by the body of a dead colleague next to him. He found himself completely trapped. He hoped and waited for rescuers to find him.

As daylight broke he began to hear voices outside his icy tomb but he could not make enough sound himself to draw their attention. During the course of the day he heard helicopters come and go until darkness fell. It was a long, cold night.

The next day more activity above him, more helicopters, and still nobody found him.

It wasn't until the third day that he was found. As he was pulled out of the snow he was only wearing a pair of light trousers and a shirt. He was suffering from hypothermia and frostbite to his extremities.

That same snowfall had landed on the roofs of classrooms at Khumjung School in the Khumbu Valley that leads up to Everest. The school hall succumbed to the weight of the snow and the roof collapsed into the room below, creating a jumbled pile of corrugated iron, timber and snow. It also pushed the drystone walls out, collapsing sections of the building into piles of rubble.

The building had originally been funded by a Japanese group, who, on hearing of the damage, sent money for it to be repaired. Unfortunately, the instructions that came with the funding seemed to get lost in translation and the work was never done.

During April 1996, I was leading a group of sixth-form boys to Everest Base Camp, Kala Pathar and the Gokyo Valley. Included in the itinerary was a week at Khumjung School to produce a play to be performed in the school hall.

Khumjung School is important in the Khumbu. It is the first school that Ed Hillary built when he established the Sir Edmund Hillary Himalayan Trust, and has become a flagship for his education programme in the Everest region.

With the school hall out of use, I looked for alternative venues within the school. There were no classrooms big enough. At the end of the school compound there is a natural amphitheatre, which would have been ideal, were it not still full of snow.

Abandoning the idea of doing some drama, we looked into the possibility of repairing the school hall. We did not have any tools. Nor did we have any building skills. If we could get the local community involved, we could, possibly, work together.

We set about the task of clearing the debris from inside the hall. We soon found inquisitive Sherpas coming to see what we were up to. Soon, they produced tools and half a dozen men came to help. They did more than help; they took over, which was just what we, unskilled labourers, needed to happen. Any language barrier there might have been was soon overcome by the use of mime.

While half the group worked on the dismantling of the building, the other half spent time with the children in the classrooms, talking to them about their home, school and the sort of life they led. The conversation never dried up as the Nepali children had plenty of questions to ask. They also taught us Sherpa songs and dances.

Outside, we played football with them, but they always had the upper hand, being used to playing football at 4000m!

All the time the work continued on the building, separating the corrugated iron from the timbers, straightening any bent sheets so that they could be used again, sawing off broken ends of timber so they, too, could be reused. The stones were piled up around the outside of the building ready for reuse.

By the time everything was ready for rebuilding, it was almost time for us to continue with our trek. Our building skills were limited, so it was better that we left the Sherpas to do it. We had done our bit; we had set the ball in motion and managed to get the local community to take responsibility for their school. We left them happily reconstructing the hall.

On our way up to Gokyo we passed through Pangka and the site of the campsite destroyed six months previously. Flattened tents still lay strewn across the ground. Cooking pots still lay where the avalanche deposited them, as were items of personal kit.

I sat on a rock surveying the scene. Looking up at the slope above, it was hard to imagine that it could cause so much damage, so much grief. There was a very sombre atmosphere and I could almost hear the cries of those swept away and buried by the avalanche. It provided a stark reminder how, sometimes, our lives are held by a very slender thread and that in this environment anything can happen to break that thread.

The rest of the trek was a huge success, although the trek up to Gokyo village was difficult in deep snow. There was a crust to the surface, but it was not very strong. I spent a lot of time following a porter, who on many occasions fell through the crust, only stopping when the base of his doko hit the snow. Without me behind him he would have struggled to get out, first having to detach himself from his load, climb out, pick up the load, reposition it on his back with the head strap across his forehead, continue for a few steps for it to happen again and again. At least with me and others behind him, we could pick him up and set him quickly on his way.

Falling through the snow was fun for the first few times but it was exhausting. It must have happened at least fifty times on the walk up the valley and by the time we reached Gokyo we were truly shattered.

The successes included an ascent of Gokyo Ri (5357m), affording us far-reaching views, including a very clear view of Everest. We then travelled around into the Khumbu, where we climbed Kala Pathar (5643m) and visited a very busy Everest Base Camp. Sadly, 1996 was the year that eight climbers died during a blizzard.

The final success was returning to Khumjung to see the school hall reconstruction completed and in full working order. While we were higher up the valley, Ed Hillary had been on his annual visit to the school and was pleased to see it restored.

A bonus for us when we returned to Kathmandu was that we were able to meet Sir Edmund Hillary and George Lowe. They were both on the successful Everest '53 Expedition. While Ed Hillary and Tenzing Norgay reached the summit, I don't think they would have done it without George Lowe having spent eleven days cutting steps up the Lhotse face, in order to pave the way for them.

They showed their gratitude to us for prompting the Khumjung School repairs by spending time talking and sharing some of their stories. We felt truly privileged.

CHAPTER 4

—

FUN AND GAMES

It is inevitable, when travelling with seventeen-year-olds, that sport is never far from their leisure activity. It can be a great icebreaker at a first meeting; it draws people together with a common purpose, to beat the opposition but also, more importantly, to enjoy the encounter.

One of my first strategies was to encourage all my students to learn to juggle, something most managed to do with varying degrees of competency. Having learnt, they would take their juggling balls out to Nepal, explain that everybody in the UK can juggle, and commence teaching the Sherpas and porters how to do it. It didn't take long. We gave them all their own juggling balls and, from then on, every spare moment was spent mastering the art. We would see balls popping up from behind a tent as a seated cross-legged porter mastered the skills. Soon, they were better than us, and teaching us a few tricks.

Football was a firm favourite and, wherever there was a reasonably flat space and somebody had a football, a game always took off. Inevitably, it became an international event with a lot of pride at stake. We English, the originators of football, wanted to show that we were still world-beaters. The Nepalese were keen to show us that they had learnt a thing or two.

Games were never evenly matched, and our trekkers might be forgiven for thinking they had the upper hand. They had boots on, enabling them to run freely on stony ground. They were twice as tall as their opponents and, probably, a lot older. It did not matter how heavily the odds were stacked against the barefooted, barely teenage opposition, they always had the upper hand, acclimatised to altitude.

There was a limit as to how fast and how far we could run in the thinner atmosphere of the Khumbu. There was no way that we could keep up with the nimble-footed children who found dodging around our cumbersome bodies so easy. It was a salutary lesson to learn that, however good you were on the King's School playing fields, you were no match for the children who lived in this environment.

Adults, when they think they can play football, are worse. At least, at sea level, the students can play. We played a game on the Manaslu Circuit trek in 2011 where we had to have rolling substitutes to allow players to come off the field of play, connect their finger to a pulse oximeter, and only return to play once their heartbeat had reduced sufficiently.

Being on the Indian subcontinent meant that cricket was always a possibility. Every Indian and Nepali male can play and we had some hugely contested games against our Indian crew in Ladakh. There were always some exceptional cricketers among the crew, who had a superb eye for the ball when batting, and could really make a tennis ball fizz when bowling.

The games when each team was a "national" side were very one-sided and the outcome was easily predicted. The best games were those where we mixed the nationalities together in each team, creating a real bond between the group and crew.

Some of the most memorable games were those that took place in Lukla at the end of a trek in the Everest region. Unfortunately, those games are a thing of the past, as security deems it a risk to allow it to happen anymore.

These games took place on the apron of Lukla Airport before it was tarmacked. After the last flight, usually around lunchtime, the runway and apron would be deserted. From our camp, at the top end of the runway, we could keep an eye out for the signal that a game was about to start. Men would begin to gather. One would arrive with a wooden crate, about the size of a set of stumps. Another would bring out a bag of flour to mark the crease. A couple of bats would appear and somebody would produce a new cricket ball.

The boys in camp, watching this, would begin to stir, stretch a few muscles, swing an arm or two, prior to descending onto the runway to throw down a challenge. Hands would be shaken, a coin tossed, and battle would commence.

The matches played would be limited to twelve overs each side, and, providing the ball was not lost, and security hadn't kicked us off the apron, we could easily play a three-match series before bad light would stop play.

These were extremely competitive matches, the more so because the surface was so unpredictable. It wasn't a flat, well-prepared wicket but a stony surface of protruding edges that sent the ball all over the place.

In 1998, we fared well in the test series, largely due to the input of two exceptional cricketers, Dan Cullen and Charlie Daniell, who both hit numerous sixes that bounced on the corrugated roofs of the surrounding buildings. It wasn't easy, though, as the Sherpas produced some good players who could match Dan and Charlie for skill. Of course, the Sherpas had home advantage, understanding the strange quirks of the pitch much better than us.

Shortly after that well-matched series, the apron and runway were given a smooth surface and the authorities put up security fencing around the airport and would not allow cricketers to stray onto the area. This coincided with the Maoist insurgency, so, perhaps, it should have been expected.

In India, one of the girls on the trip was having difficulty using the toilet tent. This had to be rectified before the situation became serious. The other girls suggested they have sole use of the camping site while they helped her to overcome her phobia. Would I take the boys off for a game to keep them out of the way? What game could we play? The environment was not conducive to football or cricket, the area not being big enough, just a plateau with a drop down to the river on three sides.

Thinking on my feet, I took a Frisbee with me and invented a simple but enjoyable game. Two teams faced each other about twenty metres apart. The object of the game was to throw the Frisbee as hard as possible at the opposing team, while maintaining control of its flights. It could not go above head height. Those on the receiving end had to defend their line at all cost. If not, the throwers were given a point. The team receiving then had their go.

It also became a bit tactical because each team would be looking for weaknesses in the opposition defence, while also wanting to ensure that their own weaknesses were strengthened.

It developed into a really enjoyable challenge and the game lasted a lot longer than the girls required.

It is a game that has continued to be enjoyed by subsequent groups.

In 2004, following a trek in Tibet, we were spending a week in Kathmandu, working on a couple of projects in a school and in a home for disabled children. As part of the school project at Sapta Gandaki Boarding School, I suggested we have a volleyball match with a trophy for the victors. Unfortunately, this only involved the boys in the group and not the girls.

My group of six-foot boys were confident that they would have the upper hand over a team of younger, five-foot boys. Their confidence was their downfall as the Sapta Gandaki team trounced us and were fully deserving of the trophy that I had taken out from Worcester. My boys took it well and a firm bond between the two groups was the real winner.

There is another sport that girls tend not to get involved with, while boys cannot resist. That is snowball fights.

Whenever we reached the snowline, seventeen-year-old boys suddenly become seven-year-olds. They run around gathering snowballs, pelting each other and trying to outwit each other.

Meanwhile, the girls sit on the stools taken from the mess tent and "tut" at the boys' antics, watching them exhaust themselves.

It is hardly surprising that, when a big day follows such games, it is the girls who succeed, who reach the summit, while the boys are too exhausted from throwing snowballs. On the whole the boys do reach the summit, but they do not perform as well as the rested girls.

Sometimes the snow can work in our favour. In 1999, when I first did the Annapurna Circuit, there was very little snow and the 4500 feet of descent from the Thorang La was a knee-jerking experience. In 2002 there was plenty of snow, so we utilised our survival bags and bin liners, anything that would give us sliding capability. We tobogganed 3000 feet of the descent, making it much quicker, a lot more comfortable on the knees, and a lot of fun.

These activities, whatever they were, always involved our hosts or specific members of the community, and, whatever the outcome, it always succeeded in bringing us closer together, creating friendships that would survive the test of time and distance.

CHAPTER 5

—

NOBBY'S VIEW

In 1998 I started to dream of a millennium project and, while I was up in Gokyo, a suggestion was put to me. Above the Fifth Lake, right at the foot of the world's sixth highest peak, Cho Oyu, is an unnamed, unclimbed peak. Why don't you do that? An unnamed, unclimbed peak! Wow! How exciting would that be? Following the line of the glacier towards Cho Oyu, I could see the dark outline of a rocky peak. That looked just the ticket. Looking at the map, it certainly did not have a name, but it was given the height of 5553m.

What is more, we would be allowed to name it. How could that be so? I was told that if I put in a written application it would be presented to the appropriate government department and they would be sure to agree. As I write this I realise just how green I was, how wet behind the ears, how gullible. But I was excited and when you are excited you tend to lose all sense of reality.

Having taken photographs of my peak, I put together a trek and presented it enthusiastically to a group of pupils and parents, who, like me, were sucked into the idea.

Over the next eighteen months we trained hard, including

carrying out a relay from John o'Groats to Land's End. We raised money for charitable projects in Nepal and by the time Easter 2000 came along we were ready for the challenge.

Before we could set out, there was just one more thing to do. I managed, on one of the training exercises, to pick up a piece of Lakeland slate. This I had carved, ready for leaving on the summit, with the following:

कइन्ग्स पेअक्
Rajako Himal (King's Peak)
April 2000

As often happens on trek, illness began to strike on the second day, which happens to be one of the hardest days of the trek, the climb up to Namche Bazaar. It is usually the result of something eaten or drunk in Kathmandu. On this occasion two boys were struggling with the pace and altitude in their debilitated state; it soon became clear that Namche Hill was going to be beyond their capability.

Settling them in a lodge in Benkar with one of the medics, the rest of us carried on to Monjo and then the long, steep climb up through the forest, thankfully reaching Namche Bazaar as weariness and altitude were beginning to affect us all.

While we took advantage of an acclimatisation day in Namche, enjoying the shops and cafes, the two patients, having recovered, took a very leisurely climb up the hill to join us.

Namche Bazaar, the capital of the Khumbu, is a most fascinating place. It sits in a natural bowl, with steep sides going up on three sides and a steep slope (the one we had climbed) falling away on the fourth side. All the buildings are arranged in contouring arcs around the bowl. Our campsite was at the top of the village adjacent to the Sherpa Heritage Museum. It was a great place to camp, but it did mean that after every visit into town we had a heart-pounding, lung-busting climb back to camp.

The remainder of the trek, while still challenging, did not test us quite as hard as that first major climb. The days tended to be shorter, the distances attainable and the height gain less severe.

Another acclimatisation stop in Machermo gave us an opportunity to explore the possibility that the Sherpa legend of Machermo could be true. The story surrounds the reporting, in 1974, of a Yeti attack on a young yak herder and her herd. She was thrown to one side by a five-foot Abominable Snowman, who then went on to kill several of her yaks. It's an interesting story, and it was reported in *The Times*, but whether there is any truth in it, nobody can honestly say. It is like the Loch Ness monster. I think we would all like there to be some truth in the story as it adds to the fascination of our world.

Having acclimatised, we continued, eventually arriving at Gokyo, a small seasonal village catering for trekkers. Behind the village the lateral moraine of the Ngozumba Glacier rises steeply, affording dramatic views onto its undulating and rocky surface to the mountains beyond. At the head of the valley we could see our ultimate goal, King's Peak, standing out rocky and grey against the white backdrop of the world's sixth highest mountain, Cho Oyu.

Before we could attempt that, we had the ascent of Gokyo Ri to overcome. Gokyo Ri (5357m) is a stunning climb in its own right and affords fantastic views of Everest and all the high Himalayan peaks in a 360° circle.

Rising before daybreak on a very cold, crisp, starlit morning, we set off on the ascent. Having crossed the end of the lake, the climb is steep for the first hour or so. We had not gone very far when one of the team slowed to a virtual stop. He was not coping well with the altitude and the early start. As I had been to the summit of Gokyo Ri before, it was only right that I should take him down to camp.

While he rested in his tent, I could watch the progress of the group until the slope began to flatten out and they were taken from view. It was while I was watching them that another, a girl this time, was brought into camp by one of the Sherpas. She, too, was feeling the effect of the altitude.

I could not help but envy the group heading for the summit. The conditions were perfect – not a cloud in the sky. They were going to get exceptional views from the summit.

As is usual in the Himalayas, as the morning wore on, the cloud began to rise up from the valleys below. Eventually, the group began to filter back, tired but very satisfied with their morning's achievement and the rewards it provided.

Naturally, the excited lunchtime conversation was all about their experiences of the morning. I began to feel sorry for the two who had been forced to return. I was also concerned about their ability to climb King's Peak, which, if they didn't, they would have nothing positive to say about the two climbs. So, after lunch, I whispered in their ears, "Let's go for a walk."

By now the cloud was a full blanket above our heads and the temperature was dropping. I explained that we were going to head up towards Gokyo Ri, but we were going to do it at a leisurely pace, without any pressure to get to the summit; they could turn round at any point if they felt uncomfortable. We were taking one Sherpa with us.

With the minimum of fuss, we left camp. I didn't want the others to know where we were going or what we were doing, as that would have added to the pressure. Very slowly we edged our way up the steep section, gradually making progress. While they found it hard, at no time did they really struggle; it was as much a mental challenge as a physical one.

By the time we reached the crest of the hill, where the slope began to ease, the cloud was upon us and there were a few flakes of snow drifting around. Undeterred, we continued, and after three hours we reached the summit. Unfortunately, there were no views to be had but we all had the satisfaction of succeeding. Even if they do not make it to the summit of King's Peak, they can still hold their heads up high, having climbed Gokyo Ri. They were tired, very tired, but their energy levels gradually improved as we began our descent in increasing snow flurries.

By the time we reached camp it was dark and everybody knew

where we had been and were just as happy that we had succeeded as they had been for themselves in the morning.

The following morning we headed on up the valley, deeper into the mountains. Most visitors to the region go no further than Gokyo, which sits on the shores of the Third Lake. We were heading up to set up camp beyond the Fifth Lake, an area rarely visited. On the way we stopped to admire the view from Scoundrels View, which gave us uninterrupted vistas of the south-west face of Everest, the South Col and Lhotse.

Base Camp was a dried-up lakebed with a glacial moraine hiding King's Peak from our view. In the afternoon I climbed the moraine to have a look at the route up. It was a steep, continuous climb with what looked like a boulder field, for the last section.

Base Camp was cold, and a combination of that, and a mixture of excitement and apprehension, meant a restless, largely sleepless night. Bed tea arrived at 4.15am and was followed a few minutes later by a steaming bowl of porridge.

Under cover of darkness, we left camp and climbed the moraine before descending to the foot of King's Peak. It was extremely cold, with fingers and toes suffering the most. Stopping for more than a minute or two was not an option, so we maintained a slow but steady pace. Gradually, the sun began to rise over the mountains to the east, casting an orange glow onto the white peaks around us. As soon as the sun's rays hit us, we were injected with a new energy as warmth coursed its way through our bodies, reaching the extremities.

At the top of the ridge we came across the boulder field, which, now we were on it, was much bigger than we first thought.

We could now see the summit. Hang on: those are prayer flags on the summit! We clearly were not the first. The thought that somebody had been here before was a huge disappointment and for a while I felt very negatively towards the mountain. But then you look around, appreciate where you are, what you are achieving, and you begin to realise it does not matter. It was at this point in the climb that Dorje, our sirdar, remembered being here with an American group twenty years previously.

We clambered our way over the boulders and after about four hours we reached the flag-strewn summit. It was quite a tight fit for such a large group as the summit fell away steeply on all sides. The views were outstanding.

On the summit, we placed our Lakeland slate sign and, also, a book that we had all written in with a little biography of each of us and a paragraph on our hopes for the future. Each contributor included a passport photo. The book was carefully wrapped in polythene to protect it from the elements and deposited in a crevice in the rocks. There was a note included, inviting anybody who found it to add their own comments.

After forty-five minutes or so on the summit, we began to head down, picking our way carefully over the boulders. I was trailing at the back of the group, really savouring my time on the mountain now that I had overcome the shock of not being the first.

As we approached the lower quarter of the mountain, we spotted a lone figure making his way up. As we met, he said, "'Ave yow bin up Nobby's View?" with a strong Black Country accent.

I didn't know what to say. I was lost for words. Nobby's View? "Don't you mean King's Peak?"

"Nah, this is Nobby's View," he retorted with confidence. "Where are you guys from?" he asked.

"Worcester," I replied.

"Ah, I'm from just up the road from yow. I'm from Stourbridge. Small world, 'init?"

With that he headed on up Nobby's View while we continued our descent from King's Peak!

6
—

DRAMA ON THE SINGALILA RIDGE

Nowadays, a great deal of emphasis is placed upon risk assessment: taking consideration of all possibilities and having policies to cover all those possibilities. I agree, it is very important to plan beforehand, to know what to do when something goes wrong. But it rarely works out as it does on paper. There is nothing more important than how you manage a situation, when it arises, out in the field.

In 2001 I was leading an adult group on a two-part trek that would take us close to Kangchenjunga, at 8586m the world's third highest mountain. The first part of the journey would take us from Nepal, across the border into West Bengal and journey up to Darjeeling. Having enjoyed the Englishness of Darjeeling, we travelled towards the Himalayas and embarked on the first part of the trek along the Singalila Ridge, a ridge that formed the boundary between Nepal to the west and India to the east. Having travelled as far along the ridge as we were allowed, we were to drop down to the town of Rimbik, whereupon we would drive into Sikkim, for the second part of the trek that would take us up to the Goecha La Pass at 4940m, affording us fantastic views of Kangchenjunga.

Sometimes, plans change!

It was a Sunday morning and we had just reached the high point of the Singalila Ridge. It was still early enough for the air to be clear. To the north was the wall of the Kangchenjunga massif.

Although the ridge carried on for some distance, it led into a restricted area, forcing us to make a two-day descent into the small town of Rimbik, before driving into Sikkim and starting part two of the trek.

We had not gone far on our descent when one of the group let out a yell of pain. Looking round, Caroline was on the ground, crying in some considerable pain. Normally, we would have had a doctor on trip but this was the first occasion we had travelled without one. We had a physiotherapist with us and I had my remote first aid qualification. It was looking quite serious and all the symptoms pointed towards knee ligament damage. Caroline kept feeling dizzy with pain and it took some time for the cocktail of painkillers we administered to take effect.

What could have caused such an accident? The slope was quite gentle and there did not seem to be any tricky bits. It transpired that Caroline had put her foot into a shallow groove in the grassy path. What she did not realise was that there was an exposed tree root crossing the groove, into which her heel lodged, so that when she tried to move it forward her foot remained while the leg tried to go, bending the knee the wrong way.

This was potentially a very tricky situation; we were two days' walk away from Rimbik. There would be no help coming to meet us. We were going to have to manage this ourselves and make sure that Caroline suffered as little as possible in the process.

After nearly an hour assessing and managing the situation, including immobilising the knee as much as we could with tight bandages, one of the Sherpas, Guhli, was designated to carry Caroline out. He is normally a porter but had been promoted for this trek, and was probably chosen for this task because he was the tallest of the Sherpas. I happened to have a couple of silk scarves with me, which we tied together to make a large sling. The Sherpa would put it across his forehead, while the other end of the loop was placed around Caroline's bottom to create a seat. It took some time to organise it and to get Caroline into a comfortable position so that she could sit in the sling. And, so, the slow process of going down the trail began. One of the problems was that Caroline was taller than her Sherpa and her legs dangled perilously close to the ground. As much as the Sherpa was careful, twisting his body to avoid her feet touching the ground, the inevitable happened occasionally, resulting in a scream of pain each time.

It was clear that this was not going to work, certainly for two days. We requested that one of our pack ponies be sent back up the hill to give Caroline a more comfortable descent.

It took about three hours for the pony to come back up the track to meet us, during which time we had made reasonable, if slow, progress. The Sherpa doing the carrying certainly earned his money that day, not once complaining or straying from his task of getting Caroline down the mountain as safely and as comfortably as he could.

The pony certainly added more pace to the descent and it was marginally more comfortable, although Caroline had to sit with her right foot pointing forwards, while the left sat in the stirrup.

It took us the whole of the day to descend into camp, which was well established by the time we arrived. There was no way that Caroline was going to cope in a tent so we went to visit the nearest house across the meadow from the camp. There, we explained the situation and asked if they had a spare bed for the night. They didn't, but they were happy to vacate their beds so that Caroline and Tim, her husband, could have some relative comfort together. Their hosts moved themselves out onto the veranda for the night.

They settled for the night and the rest of us all ventured into the village of Gorky. It was while we were in the village that I learnt of another medical problem. Roger came up to me and dropped his shorts to show me a tick that had buried its head into his groin! Knowing that ticks, wherever they are, let alone in a sensitive region, can cause trouble, we needed to deal with it. Dropping his shorts in the middle of the village caused quite a stir and we soon had a crowd gathered around us.

We needed some alcohol, but we also needed an explanation. The language barrier was proving to be just that, a barrier. The audience grew as Roger stood there in his underpants, with his shorts around his ankles. Villagers chipped in with suggestions, producing lots of sniggers.

Finally the request for alcohol was understood and one of the villagers ran off in search, returning a few minutes later with several bottles of beer. Not wishing to offend, we drank the beer while trying to explain the need for some tweezers. All the time the smiling crowd increased, partly because Roger, with his shorts, still round his ankles, was enjoying the attention.

Eventually, the villager, who seemed to understand the need for tweezers, returned carrying the biggest pair of fire tongs I have ever seen. We all fell about laughing, which was a great antidote to the main stress of the day and the stress that was yet to come. Not only could we relieve Roger of his tick; we could easily inflict a lot of collateral damage!

More beer was produced but we were getting no further with the tick removal, until one of the Sherpas came by, took out a lighter, and began teasing the tick – I repeat, tick – with it before nipping it out with his forefinger and thumb. As soon as Roger pulled his shorts up, the crowd lost interest in him and began to drift off.

The following morning Caroline and Tim set off early, ahead of the main group, hoping to have a pain-free journey down to Rimbik. Having a bed to sleep on rather than a tent to crawl into had been a godsend and they had had a reasonably comfortable night, although Caroline was never without pain.

It was a delightful walk, initially through forests of pine trees and then steeply terraced farmland. We even included a lunchtime river swim.

By late afternoon, we arrived at the Sherpa Hotel in Rimbik, and you could be forgiven for thinking that now we could sort

Caroline out, get her treatment, make phone calls and arrange for her and Tim's repatriation, as that now seemed to be the only sensible course of action. It wasn't that simple. We had walked into day one of a three-day, all-inclusive strike in West Bengal. Nothing was open, nothing was allowed to move and, if the rules of the strike were broken, there was the threat of violence. Had we not got a medical emergency, we could have managed it but our priority, now that we had reached civilisation, was to get the best possible outcome for Caroline.

We had three choices:

1.   We could sit it out in the hotel and wait for the strike to end. This would not only be uncomfortable for Caroline but it would have an impact upon the rest of our itinerary.
2.   We could walk about seven miles through the jungle to the Sikkim border, beyond which the strike had no impact. This was not an option as it would be much too difficult and painful for Caroline.
3.   We could make our escape in vehicles, under the cover of darkness, and hope that we did not get stopped by strike activists.

We managed to arrange a meeting with the local strike leader, who, to be fair, understood the predicament we were in. He advised us that, should we decide on option 3, he would guarantee our safe journey through his area. He could not guarantee that we would be treated the same in areas outside his control. He was at pains to tell us that we would not come to any harm but our vehicles would be seized and set on fire, leaving us stranded.

With information gathered we held a group meeting to decide our plan. The vast majority voted for option 3, the night-time escape. It was worth the risk, and, if we were stopped, we could plead that they, at least, allow Caroline to continue with Tim.

After a rather subdued early evening meal we all retired to our rooms to pack and to try to catch up on a bit of sleep before our clandestine departure. Sleep did not come very easily.

At 11.00pm two buses and a jeep pulled up outside the hotel. One of the buses was playing loud music. The front bus was for all our kit and the crew. The Land Cruiser behind was for Caroline and Tim and behind that was the second bus for the rest of the group. We quietly and efficiently loaded our kit and then ourselves aboard the vehicles ready for a midnight departure. Still the music played at full volume, causing us some alarm and concern.

On leaving Rimbik, remarkably without attracting any unwanted attention, the road descended steeply through a series of U-bends. It was pitch black outside, but it was just possible to see that the banks on either side of the road rose steeply.

Suddenly, we came to an abrupt stop. We could hear shouting and looking beyond the windscreen of our bus, we could see people running around at the head of the convoy. There was a lot of shouting. Each of us was beginning to fear the worst. We had been stopped and this was going to be the end of the journey, for now.

Soon the commotion died down and our crew could be seen climbing back into the bus. There seemed to be no attempt to keep quiet. We were off again and back on came the music. A huge sense of relief passed around the bus. We later learnt that we had not been ambushed but a large trunk of bamboo had fallen across the road. The front bus with the crew in had driven straight into it, smashing the windscreen. The commotion had been the clearing away of the bamboo. That bus continued without a windscreen for the rest of the journey! It must have been uncomfortably cold, particularly for the driver.

At about four in the morning we crossed the border into Sikkim. We had managed the journey without further incident.

Another hour, and we came across a small settlement where we could stretch our legs, get some breakfast, and, more importantly, transfer Caroline and Tim into a vehicle with Sikkim licence plates. The significance of this was that Caroline needed to get to Nepal by travelling through West Bengal. A vehicle with Sikkim plates was exempt from the rules pertaining to the strike; she would be allowed clear passage.

After breakfast, we said our farewells to Caroline and Tim, wishing them a safe return to the UK, while we ventured deeper into Sikkim.

Caroline and Tim's journey was quite remarkable. They managed to get through to the Nepali border without incident and onto a plane in Bhadrapur, which took them to Kathmandu. There, they were met and taken to the hotel while their international flight was confirmed. Caroline was in considerable discomfort but she was well looked after.

On the flight back to the UK she was given preferential treatment. It appeared there might be a problem when they got back to Heathrow. None of the family were able to come to meet them and Tim was all for getting the train back to Worcester. Caroline wanted an ambulance.

On arrival at Heathrow, Tim stuck to his guns, put Caroline onto a trolley and waited to collect their luggage. It was while waiting that Caroline's brother came by, purely by coincidence, having just flown in from Amsterdam. More importantly, his estate car was parked at the airport, so Caroline had a more comfortable journey than planned.

As soon as they reached Worcester, Caroline was taken to the hospital, where she learnt she had broken her leg. In fact, not just once; there were six breaks to the knuckle of the tibia, just below the knee. She was on the operating table on the Wednesday, having had the accident the previous Sunday morning.

Caroline is a remarkable woman. Despite being in great pain and discomfort, she showed tremendous strength and resilience in extremely difficult and worrying circumstances.

7

HITTING THE HEADLINES

With student trips there was always an eighteen-month training period when the students would come together for specific activities. One of these was a long-distance trek with backup support in the form of moveable camps, with minibuses to transport kit and camp managers. We tried to replicate the experience they would have on their eventual expedition using a full support crew.

In the summer of 2001 we decided to walk the length of Wales from Holyhead to the Gower, taking in some decent ascents in Snowdonia and the mountains of mid-Wales.

All was going well until we reached a campsite just north of Plynlimon. There, something happened that sparked off a chain of remarkable events. One of the minibuses got a puncture in a rear wheel. That, in itself, should not have been a problem. It was simply a case of replacing it with the spare. But the spare could not be released from its housing underneath the rear of the bus, the nuts holding it having seized completely. As hard as we tried, with the limited tool selection we had it could not be released. We had to call the AA, who came to the camp and, after much effort, managed to release the spare wheel and put it in the place of the punctured wheel. Having changed the

33

wheel for us, Mr AA left us with the warning that, until the puncture was repaired, we were technically illegal. It must be a priority. It was going to have to be high on our list of jobs to do the next day.

The following morning, a staff member who had his car with him drove round to the next designated campsite in order to walk towards us and meet somewhere on Plynlimon. Before we managed to get started, I received a call from him to say that he had come across footpath closure signs.

The UK had recently had a serious outbreak of foot and mouth disease, which had closed huge swathes of the countryside. We had assumed that, because the outbreak was now over, the paths would all be open. The last thing we wanted to do was upset the farming community in the areas we were walking through, so we agreed to meet in Borth on the coast just north of Aberystwyth. There we would reassess the situation and decide on a plan of action.

Visiting the tourist information office, we looked at the possibility of following the coast around to St David's. It looked a good alternative and would take about the same length of time as walking down the mountain spine of Wales. We bought all the necessary maps, having first checked with the tourist information staff that the coastal path was open.

Having made the decision, how were we going to manage the new and immediate situation? We needed to fix the minibus tyre to make its use legal. We had to find a campsite that would take us at short notice. A phone call to a campsite in Llanrhystud sorted that problem out. We had to shuffle vehicles around and we had to be sure that we had the right pupil:staff ratio to ensure that they were safe. We had fourteen students and four adults, one of whom was not a staff member but a doctor who would be joining us on the expedition in Nepal. John had to take his car to the finish. I had to get the minibus to a garage in Aberystwyth. We had to leave the other minibus at the start point of the new route, Clarach, for collection later. Only twelve students could walk as we could only have two adults walking, so my son, Stephen, and one other joined me.

The plan was that, having set the group off from Clarach, I would drive the minibus and the tyre, with the two boys, to a garage in Aberystwyth, leave the wheel at the garage for later collection, and then drive in convoy with John to Llanrhystud. From there we would walk north along the coast path to meet the group heading south.

All that done, the four of us started walking north. As we were doing so, I received a phone call from my wife, Angela, walking with the group, to say that they had come across footpath closure signs and were heading south along the beach. They had done everything that was required of them in the situation; they had checked on the map that there was a path up from the beach. That had been confirmed by asking a local if that was the case. They had also checked the tide times and the next high tide was not until 10.15pm. It was now early afternoon. Having been assured that they were in control of the situation, I told them to continue but to keep me informed of progress.

Ironically, we also came across footpath closure signs and, because we could not find a coastal route, we headed further inland. By late afternoon, we reached Aberystwyth and took advantage of a little light refreshment on the seafront. We saw no point in the boys doing the last three miles to pick up the second bus, so we left them to look after our rucksacks while John and I ran over the cliffs to Clarach.

It was only as we approached the minibus that John realised the keys were in his rucksack. This now put us under a bit of time pressure. I needed to get to the garage before it closed.

While my colleague embarrassingly ran back to collect the keys, I, having missed lunch, decided to buy myself a pork pie. I was just munching away on it when my phone rang. It was Angela. There was no path up from the beach! There had been a landslide. They had walked eight miles over a rocky, ankle-twisting coast. One boy was struggling and there was no way they could walk back.

"You make a decision," I told Angela gruffly, realising the consequences of dialling 999.

With the group sitting on rocks at the foot of the cliffs, Angela went out onto the rocks, in order to get a better signal, and called the emergency services. Their immediate reaction was to summon the coastguard.

In the meantime, John returned with the keys to the minibus. We drove round to the garage and picked up the repaired wheel, picked up the two boys and drove down to Llanrhystud. I was anxious for news.

I needed to be occupied so I decided that the four of us at camp should put up the tents ready for the group arriving after their adventure. While we were doing so, Stephen suddenly said, "Dad, what are all those people doing?"

Between the campsite and the beach there was a levee and there were about three hundred people standing on it looking out to sea. Beyond, we could see two lifeboats heading towards the area where the group were waiting, although we could not see them. It was just after six and all the people in their caravans had heard it on the news and had come out to watch the scene unfold before them.

At Llanrhystud there is a small river estuary and I could see that the lifeboats were coming ashore on the wrong side of the estuary. I quickly got in the minibus and drove round there. Another crowd of onlookers had gathered, along with three television crews. The group were just being transferred from the offshore lifeboat to the inshore and then carried by hunky lifeboat men from the inshore boat to the beach. I was pleased to see that the group were in good spirits but I was more concerned about the publicity that was going to follow. As they were brought ashore I instructed them to go to the minibus, climb aboard and talk to no one.

All safely ashore and seated in the minibus, I drove round to the camp, where, fortunately, all the tents were erected. The television crews were positioned now on the levee overlooking our camp. I positioned the minibus so that they got out from the side away from the cameras and told them to go straight to their tents, where we would give them some hot drinks and a snack.

We went about our business, ignoring the onlookers, and

eventually they drifted off back to their caravans. All except the TV crews.

Eventually one of the reporters came up to me and said, "Is nobody going to talk to us?"

"No," I replied. "All you need to know is that the appropriate action was taken at the appropriate time for the appropriate reasons."

"Will you say that on air?" he asked.

"No," I replied again.

"Why not?"

"Because you will then ask me a question that I am not prepared to answer."

"OK. When can we release this nationally?" he asked.

"I would prefer to speak to the parents first before they see their children on the television news."

"When will that be?"

"Hopefully, I will speak to them all this evening."

He was beginning to get on my nerves by now.

"If I give you a ring at 10.00pm, do you think you will have done it by then?"

"Give me a ring and I will let you know." I said, turning away to get on with more important things.

With that he and the television crews left, realising they were not going to get any more out of me.

Before I could phone the parents I had to be sure I knew exactly the sequence of events. Having called for the coastguard, it soon became apparent that they could not safely get to the group and bring them up the cliff. Hence the lifeboat call-out. Unfortunately, the closest lifeboat in Aberystwyth was being painted, so the one from New Quay, much further down the coast, had to come. The group, being on the beach, were not accessible to the offshore lifeboat, hence the need for the inshore to pick up and transfer. This added significant time to the whole process, giving news teams plenty of time to get staff to the scene.

The lifeboat crew, made up of three hunky young men,

thoroughly enjoyed the call-out. It was 27 July and this was their first call-out since January, so they were up for a bit of fun. Reassuringly, Angela was told that she had done exactly the right thing, by both the lifeboat crew and by the coastguard who met them on the shore.

I spent the evening phoning the parents, all of whom found it amusing and at no stage expressed any concern over how their children were being looked after. It was all part of the expedition experience.

At 10.00pm the reporter phoned, as promised, and was pleased to hear that I had spoken to all the parents. He could release the news across all networks.

The outcome of this was that as we continued our walk south, down the beautiful Welsh coast, we featured on the news for three days. Clearly, not much else was happening in Wales in late July! People kept stopping the group and telling them they saw them on the news. I was asked if I was going back to school to face the music.

The reportage was ridiculous, and so much of it untrue. I was referred to as a "quick-thinking geography teacher", while another paper had the pupils being winched up by helicopters just before the incoming tide consumed them.

The only letter of complaint that the school received came from a very angry man in St David's, where we were finishing with two minibuses with the name of the school plastered all over them. He wanted to know what the school was going to do. I should be sacked for gross incompetence and the school should recompense the RLNI for the cost of the call-out.

Needless to say, we completed the walk, finishing in St David's, where, fortunately, we did not meet "Mr Angry". Nobody suffered as a result of the experience and it was a story they could dine out on with the friends and family for years.

At the start of term, I had to give a report to staff on how the situation was managed, with particular reference to managing the media. At one point, I alienated myself from the whole of the Geography Department by saying that I never thought I would hear the words "quick-thinking" and "geography teacher" in the same sentence.

You might think that would be the end of the story, but far from it. It has since reappeared at different times, in different places.

The first was while we were continuing with the walk but unbeknown to us at the time. I had told every parent of the situation, but not every parent had passed on the news to their partner. One parent was in New York on business. As he was waking up, he turned on the TV for Sky News in his hotel room to see his daughter being carried from the sea by a lifeboat man. Naturally, he had questions he wanted answering.

To show our gratitude to the RLNI, we organised a sponsored swim in the school pool, using the occasion as a team-building exercise, and raised £200. Not, perhaps, the cost of the call-out but an expression of thanks.

Six months later, we were in Nepal. We had successfully trekked around Annapurna and were spending our last few days enjoying a jungle safari in Chitwan National Park. One steamy evening we were sitting in a thatched shelter with a group of Australians.

One of them appeared to be particularly quiet, until he suddenly burst out, "I knew I'd seen you lot before. You were all rescued from a beach in Wales!"

He had seen it on Sky News in Australia. The power of the media!

You would perhaps be forgiven for thinking that that is the end of the story.

Jump forward nineteen years to 2020, a memorable year in so many ways, and one that none of us wants to see repeated. Covid-19 had really restricted our movements. Since lockdown I had been nowhere. Suddenly Angela and I had the chance of a few days in Pembrokeshire with a couple of friends who have a house in St David's. I was being introduced to fly-fishing and had been taken to a lake near Carmarthen. I wasn't having much luck with the fish but was enjoying the experience nonetheless.

Towards the end of our day at the lake a chap came over and

started chatting. At some point he mentioned that he was a retired lifeboat helmsman. I had to ask.

"Where were you stationed?"

"New Quay," he replied.

"Were you there in 2001?" I asked.

"Yes, why?"

"Do you remember a school group—" I started, but was cut off before I could finish.

"Yeah, a group of fourteen! I was the helmsman on the offshore boat. It was a great day. It increased my rescue tally from sixty-six to eighty in one day. We had to behave ourselves that day, there were so many press waiting on the shore. Had to do everything by the book." He was so animated and remembered the detail as if it had been yesterday.

He finished by suggesting that we should all meet up in New Quay for a reunion. Maybe that's something I should organise for 27 July 2021.

8

ANIMAL ENCOUNTERS

It is inevitable, wherever you travel, that you will encounter animals. Those encounters generate a whole range of emotions from fear right through to enchantment. The following pages relate a number of sightings that generated that wide range of emotions.

The Chitwan National Park, in the south of Nepal, adjoins the Indian border. We go there to see the animals that live in the park and to relax after an arduous trek in the mountains.

Following my first Everest adventure, I ended up in the Chitwan. In the mornings, despite it being a lowland, jungle environment, it can be quite chilly before the sun gets up. If you want to see animals, it is always best to get up early.

On this particular occasion, we were on a jungle walk, hoping to see tigers and rhinos. The cool morning air prompted me to wear a rather bright fleece, orange, purple and yellow! Not your normal animal stalking clothing.

We didn't come across any tigers but we did come across a lone white rhino. Our guide, armed with nothing more than a stick, pointed it out to us in the elephant grass. Now, rhinos don't have particularly good eyesight but they can pick out bright colours if they are close enough, and I was close enough. The rhino suddenly started running towards me. I can assure you that when two tons of rhino run towards you, picking up speed all the time, it is a bit scary. Where to go? What to do?

The guide shouted, "Hide behind a tree!"

I ran to the nearest tree large enough to hide behind and waited. Nothing happened. As soon as the rhino lost sight of the brightly coloured object, he lost interest, as if to say, "What was I chasing?"

It taught me a lesson not to wear brightly coloured clothes, preferring to wear muted greens on all future trips to Chitwan.

Chitwan National Park is not awash with animals, not like some of the African game reserves, where there seem to be animals wherever you look. There can be long episodes of seeing very little. Sometimes, though, after seeing nothing we are rewarded with a spectacular sight.

In 1998, we had again just completed a really successful expedition to the Everest region and were staying in a Tharu lodge on the edge of the Chitwan. One morning, we embarked on an elephant safari. This was before people started to really question the ethical nature of such activities. The elephants, we were sure, were treated well; we had seen them in their camps. They had good relationships with their mahouts and seemed perfectly happy. None was displaying those traits associated with ill-treated animals. It also gave us closer access to the wild animals in the park because rhinos cohabit with elephants and only see the elephant and not the people sitting in the howdah on its back.

On this occasion, we were using nine elephants, and, having started out together, we fanned out so, to all intents and purposes, each elephant and its passengers was alone, giving us a better chance of seeing something special.

Angela and I had an elephant to ourselves. We hadn't seen a great deal but were enjoying the ride, nevertheless. Suddenly, our elephant began to grumble from deep inside. It was getting excited. Then our mahout pointed up to a tree. There, languishing with its paws and tail dangling, was a leopard. Its large eyes were watching us intently.

The elephant continued its grumbling and began swaying its head and lifting its trunk. The leopard decided to climb down from its lofty perch. It did so by crawling backwards down the trunk of the tree, with its extended claws giving it traction. At the foot of the tree, it disappeared into the long elephant grass.

Suddenly, there was a commotion. The leopard was now in front of us and leapt up at the head of the elephant. The elephant reared up onto its hind legs, lifting its trunk in the air and trumpeting loudly. We hung on for dear life. Angela shouted, "I've only got sandals on!" as if what she was wearing on her feet would make a difference.

Having attacked (but leaving Angela's feet intact!), the leopard shot off through the long grass. The quivering grass tips gave away its direction of travel. We set off in pursuit.

The commotion attracted all the other elephants, all equally excited. The mahouts called out instructions to each other and we soon came across the leopard skulking in the long grass. Another attack by the leopard, roaring and baring its teeth before darting off, once again, through the long grass.

For the next twenty minutes or so we stalked the leopard but without success. In many respects, as exciting as the experience was, I was glad. I didn't like seeing the animal stressed, when all it was doing was trying to protect its fresh kill at the foot of the tree, where we first found it.

That initial sighting of it languishing and then pausing during its descent from the tree will live with me forever, and compensates for not seeing a tiger on any of my visits to Chitwan National Park.

While on the theme of elephants, I had a very different experience in Tanzania in 2005. We had been there to climb Mounts Meru and Kilimanjaro, following the two ascents with various safaris. We had experienced the compact nature of Manyara National Park, where some elephants had resented our being there. We had also experienced the wide, open plains of the Serengeti National Park. Our final animal encounter was at the Ngorongoro Conservation Area, in the crater of a massive volcano.

The Ngorongoro Crater is the world's largest caldera and is home to Africa's "big five" – elephant, lion, leopard, buffalo and rhino. We also saw many hippos and it is on the migratory route of wildebeest and zebra.

The crater is only accessible during the hours of daylight, so we were camping on the rim of the crater, with panoramic views across the twelve-mile diameter to the 600m walls of the other side.

We had just gone to bed and were settling down for the night when there was a bit of commotion outside. Some were voices of excitement, while others were firm instruction. The news filtered through the canvas of our tent that there was an elephant in camp. I wasn't too concerned and, as we had seen many elephants by this stage of the trip, I wasn't really that excited.

Curiosity got the better of Angela, so she got up and went out to see what was going on.

"John, John, you need to come and see this," Angela whispered back through the tent flap.

"It's only an elephant," I mumbled, rolling over and burying myself deeper into my sleeping bag.

"No, John, you need to come and see this!" insisted Angela.

"OK, OK."

I sleep naked in my sleeping bag and I didn't fancy getting dressed again, so I shuffled out in my sleeping bag and stood, holding it firmly around me. Quite a crowd had gathered. While some took photos, rangers were shouting, "No flash! No flash!"

It took a moment for my eyes to adjust but I looked in the direction of the elephant, aiming my eyes about eight feet above ground where I expected to see a head. This was no ordinary elephant. This was a bull elephant. I had to raise my eyes a further four feet to take in the enormity of this beast's head. It had a massive, bulbous forehead, huge tusks and its trunk with a girth the size of a man's waist. It was using its trunk to delicately rummage in a bin of food waste. We were told that it was capable of picking up a single pea in its trunk!

"Wow!" was all I could utter. He was magnificent. I stood there, clutching my sleeping bag, in awe.

One of the rangers turned on the headlights of his jeep to illuminate the elephant. The whites of his eyes stood out as he rummaged for food, tipping paper and cardboard onto the ground.

The rangers were still quite agitated. Elephants can quickly change their temper if goaded. They had their rifles ready just in case. Gently, they tried to ease the spectators back a little.

Soon, everything edible had been retrieved from the bin. Where would the elephant go next? Would he seek out another bin? For a while he stood there waving his trunk, taking in the scent of the assembled crowd.

Realising there was nothing more here for him, he turned and loped off into the jungle that descended towards the crater. He was truly magnificent.

In the morning, my first task was to see just how close we had been to the elephant. Pacing out the distance between our tent door and the bin, I managed eleven paces. No distance at all, particularly if the elephant took exception to us. I'm not sure what I would have done, what I could have done, standing in my sleeping bag, with, to all intents and purposes, my legs shackled by the confines of the bag.

On the ascent of Mount Meru, in Tanzania, we were staying in huts. Our guide carried a rifle at all times because of the danger we could face with wildlife, particularly the buffalo.

We were staying in the Miriakamba Hut. The adjacent toilets are a small hut with three walls, a door and no roof. In the morning, Angela took herself off to the toilet hut, and, while in there, became aware that she was not alone. She felt she was being watched. Looking up, there was a giraffe peering over the walls watching her intently. Not many people can claim to have had a giraffe as a peeping Tom!

Outside the national parks on the Terai of the south, Nepal is not blessed with a huge range of wild animals. Terraces of potatoes, onions, chard, barley and other subsistence crops have gradually replaced forest habitats. As a result, those animals that were common are becoming increasingly rare.

One of those rarities is the red panda, a much smaller cousin of the giant panda in China. In 1997, we were trekking in the Langtang Himal. We were only a couple of days into the trek, so not yet very high. We had just arrived in a damp, leech-infested camp, when somebody spotted something high up in a tree. It moved slowly from branch to branch and it took a while to see the distinctive red fur and a bushy tail against the leaves and sky above.

To our amazement, the Sherpas started throwing stones up into the tree. I think they were hoping it would move more so that we could get a better view. It certainly had that effect, except it moved as quickly as it could in order to get away from the area. We never saw it again.

The next time I saw a red panda it was in Darjeeling Zoo.

When I first went to Nepal, the skies were thick with kites and vultures. Kites are still in abundance in the skies above Kathmandu but vultures seem to be disappearing fast. The increasing use of antibiotics in farmed animals is largely to blame but when I first trekked the Annapurna Circuit, Himalayan griffon vultures were in abundance.

I had been up to the Tibetan village of Pisang on the northern side of the Annapurna range. From the lofty position of the village, I could see a lot of vulture activity on a slope about a mile away. I thought this was worth investigating.

It took a while, over mixed terrain, to get near to the activity. Not wishing to disturb the animals I approached tentatively, crouching behind juniper bushes. They seemed oblivious to me and I could now see why. There was a dead cow. There must have been at least a couple of dozen of these magnificent birds. I say magnificent, but, when their scrawny necks and heads are covered in blood, they look pretty ugly.

I modelled myself on David Attenborough, slowly and silently creeping ever closer, until I was about ten feet from the cow. As it turned out, I need not have been so cautious; they cared not a jot for me. Their only intent was to get stuck in on the fleshy remains of the cow, squabbling with each other as they fought over the tastiest morsels. One of the cow's legs twitched morbidly as they did so.

Those that had eaten stood around, too full to take to the air. Others flew in, majestically gliding in with their nine-foot wingspan, flying straight towards me. It was a really special time and I must have spent an hour just absorbed in their company.

On most treks in the Himalayas we get a camp follower in the form of a dog. They latch on to a group in the knowledge that there is a kitchen tent with many possible opportunities for scraps. Dogs in Nepal have to be opportunists, otherwise they would starve to death.

As we started the trek into Langtang, one such dog joined us. He was an attractive dog with floppy ears and a winning expression. During the day, there would be little interaction, except when we stopped at a lodge for tea or stopped for lunch, when there would be ample opportunity for a thrown titbit. At night he would hang around the kitchen tent but when we went to bed, which was quite early in the evening, the dog would seek shelter in one or other of our tent porches.

The dog came all the way up the Langtang Valley and even joined us on the ascent of Kyangjin Ri, a sub-5000m peak affording fantastic views of the whole of upper Langtang.

The weather was never very good on this trek and we had experienced some seriously snowy days. There had been so much snow that our route out, over the Gosaikunda Pass into the Helambu Valley, was impassable, forcing us to head back down to the small town of Dunche. Dunche marks the entrance to the Langtang National Park and is connected to the rest of Nepal by a rough road, along which we would have to walk for two days in order to meet up with our transport.

The main purpose of this road is to service the national park, to get tourists in and out of the area more quickly, and to allow for the transportation of bottled water from the Dunche bottling plant.

This was the only occasion that I have ever experienced animosity towards me, or members of my group.

We were well spread out along the road, enjoying the ease of the walk, conversing or simply revelling in solitude. At a point where we had an opportunity to leave the road, we waited for the group to reassemble. We were missing Gill, Rodger and the tail-end Sherpa, Bharrath, along with the dog. There was no sign of them on the road, so Dorje sent Temba back to find them.

We waited, and we waited. No sign of them.

Eventually, after about an hour, we saw them heading towards us. They had a tale to tell. They had been ambushed at the roadside by a group of men who accused them of stealing their dog. Clearly not the case but they were being opportunists.

The situation was getting tense. After a while, Gill, who stands little nonsense, said, "I've had enough of this. We are going."

The ringleader, standing in front of her and opening up his jacket to reveal a large kukri knife, replied, "You, madam, are going nowhere."

The tension suddenly intensified.

A Nepali teacher joined the group and tried to reason with them, while Bharrath offered himself up as hostage if they let Gill and Rodger go.

The root cause of the problem appears to be the road. Before the road was built, the trekking route passed through the villages on the approach to Langtang, bringing with it trekkers who would spend money on food and accommodation. The road destroyed all that. Trekkers can now travel deeper into the mountains without ever needing to stop for refreshment or accommodation. These forsaken villagers see all the money from tourism going into the Langtang National Park and none into their communities. Many have resorted to drink, with little else to do, and it is probably the alcohol that had given them the bravado to stop a couple of tourists and their Sherpa.

As the minutes ticked by, nothing was happening until Temba appeared on the scene, when the wind seemed to deflate the sails of the kidnappers. Did Temba display an aura of authority that caught them off guard? Did any money change hands to satisfy the egos of the kidnappers? I doubt it. I suspect that they could not see themselves getting anything out of it, other than potentially, a lot of trouble.

Needless to say, it had been a scary hour or so for the three victims.

And what of the dog? He remained with us until we climbed aboard our bus two days later, when he would seek out another group to latch on to.

Travelling to Indonesia allowed me to have encounters with two iconic animals, the orang-utan and the Komodo dragon.

I was trekking through the jungle of Sumatra with a group of students and we were having regular close encounters with orang-utans. They are the most gentle of creatures. We found mothers would bring their babies to show us. All the time we were conscious of maintaining appropriate distance between them and us. Nobody has fully explained the rules to the orang-utan and not all tourists respect the rules. I did see, on one occasion, a French tourist and an orang-utan walking hand in hand on a stony riverside beach.

Not all our encounters with orang-utans were as placid as that.

As a group, we had a toy orang-utan, bought in Worcester, which was our mascot to be cared for by a different person each day. The choice of person each day was dependent upon who had done or said the silliest thing in the previous twenty-four hours.

At the side of the path, sitting in a tree just above our head height was a large male orang-utan. He was sitting peacefully watching us and even allowing us to stand and watch. Suddenly, he displayed great rage and started making very threatening motions, breaking branches off the tree and waving them around before throwing them in our direction. What was causing such a change in his behaviour? He had seen the toy orang-utan attached to a rucksack and immediately assumed we had kidnapped a baby orang-utan. This could get very nasty.

Fortunately a quick-thinking guide whipped the toy off the rucksack and stuffed it into his own, ushering us on along the path at the same time. Looking back, the large male began to calm down but it taught us to show a little more respect for these wonderful creatures.

Shortly after this incident, I was carefully descending a steep slope that had been made greasy by recent rain. I used trees on either side of the path to prevent me losing control. Many of the trees were nothing more than very tall, spindly saplings, and they would bend as I clung on to them on my downward journey. As I let go the trees would spring back. Unfortunately, one of those trees had a swarm of bees in the top of it. They did not appreciate being catapulted. The guide shouted, "Run, John!"

I moved as quickly as I could on the slippery slope but the bees were out for revenge, and I received at least a dozen stings on the face and head. Remarkably, a liberal smearing of Tiger Balm, almost immediately, took all the pain out of the stings.

At one of the camps on the same trek, we were sitting on the stony beach on the riverbank watching a troupe of about one hundred macaques playing in the trees on the other side. They were making lots of noise and were entertaining us well. Unbeknown to us, as we marvelled at their antics, there was a splinter group that had worked its way behind us and was rifling through our kit stealing anything that was edible!

The Komodo dragon lives only on four islands in the world: Komodo, Rinca, Flores and Gili Motang. I first came across Komodo Dragons when I was a child, watching David Attenborough's 1956 black and white film *Zoo Quest*. They struck me then as prehistoric creatures and nothing I have seen since has changed my mind.

You are free, providing you have a guide, to wander over these idyllic islands and you are guaranteed to come across any number of dragons, ranging in length from eight to sixteen feet. Their strong, muscular tails make up almost half of their length. They can build up a very deceptive turn of speed despite having short bow legs. But it is their heads that are the most fascinating and gruesome. Their wide mouth is full of razor-sharp teeth, capable of tearing through the thick hide of a buffalo. They, alone, are not enough to kill a buffalo. As it sinks its teeth into the flesh it injects venom that prevents a wound from coagulating. Their mouths are also full of harmful bacteria, which set off infection in the wound. As they are slobbering all the time, there is plenty of bacteria to inflict their harm. Having inflicted the damage on its victim, the dragon simply has to follow it around until it collapses. Perhaps the most sinister feature is the darting tongue, shooting out eighteen inches as it probes and discovers its surroundings.

There have been attacks on humans. In 2013, three of the wardens on Rinca Island had been bitten. The wardens live in stilted huts and the dragons often rest underneath. If the warden is not careful, and clearly three hadn't been, the dragon will take a bite at their legs as the come down the steps. Fortunately, they have all the right antidotes to ensure that no other harm comes to them, other than a painful bite.

Villages have been less fortunate in years gone by. Now that the dragons are protected, so are the villagers, who prosper quite well from living in close proximity with them. While there with a student group in 2013, we paid for and built four toilets in Komodo Village, on the premise that these would negate the need for villagers to wander beyond the village boundary to go to the toilet. In fact, we discovered that these would probably be used by cruise ship passengers as there was a very long jetty, which allowed cruise ships to dock and offload passengers.

On the whole, you are safe wandering about among the dragons, provided you have your wits about you and you do not go too close. The only time I got caught out was on a beach on Komodo Island. A dragon was walking along the beach. It was an incredible sight as it wasn't half hidden by foliage and it had a turquoise sea as a backdrop. I was keen to film it. Concentrating on the process of filming, I failed to notice that the dragon had changed course and was coming straight for me. It was only the shout of the guide that alerted me to get out of the way quickly.

On a lot of our treks we have used pack animals to carry much of our kit. In Nepal and Tibet it has been yaks that have done the work. Mostly, everything runs smoothly, but occasionally you get an obstinate yak.

In Tibet we were trekking towards Shishipangma Base Camp and we came to a river crossing. While we crossed by a narrow, flimsy bridge, the yaks had to wade through the river. One particular yak decided that he had had enough of carrying his load. Standing, mid-river, it decided to shake free of its four kitbags, and there was nobody there to stop it. After some vigorous shaking, the ropes loosened and the four bags went floating down the fast-flowing river. Sherpas, only concerned with the bags, leapt into the river and retrieved them. Three of the bags contained our sleeping bags, but, because they were so tightly packed into their stuff sacks, the water had not managed to penetrate them. The fourth bag belonged to our sirdar, Dorje, who cheerfully announced that his clothes no longer smelt!

When we went to K2, we used camels as our pack animals. They were a wonderful sight walking head to tail along the flat, wide riverbeds of this incredibly remote region. There was something biblical about seeing the camel train. Most of the camels are female but there was the odd male among them.

Camels are not always on their best behaviour, particularly when they have sex on their mind. We were camping at Chinese Base Camp and had just gone to bed. Suddenly, there was a huge commotion and we could hear fast-moving, heavy feet hitting the ground. This was followed by mighty tugs on guy ropes. Above it all, a voice rang out, "Slackbar, sort these fucking camels out!" I hasten to add, here, that our sirdar was a Uyghur called Ackbar. Unfortunately, his heart was not in his work, so he tended to disappoint us on more than one occasion.

Needless to say, the camels were sorted out and the culprit was a single male camel that had decided he was going to terrorise all the females in order to satisfy his lust, and, if it meant jumping over tents, he would do it. It is remarkable that nobody was hurt.

On another occasion, we used camels to cross one of the many rivers we came across. Some behaved better than others.

There was one that had much lighter fur than all the others and she became affectionately known as Blondie. Camels are strong animals so two people could ride together on one. David insisted on riding her and took Robin as his partner for the crossing. Unfortunately, Blondie had other ideas and spent the river crossing doing her best to ditch them both into the icy water.

Not all animals are a pleasure to encounter. When conditions are favourable, i.e. wet, leaches are an annoyance. They don't hurt and often you are not aware of them until it is too late. They latch on to you, often under your clothing, and fill themselves with your blood. There is no escape. They are in foliage at ground level, waiting for you to brush past. They hang from trees, waiting to drop on you from above. When they have had their fill, they drop off, leaving a seeping wound because they have injected an anticoagulant into the wound. They are not disease carriers and they cause you no harm. They are simply annoying.

Sri Lanka provided us with one of the funniest experiences of the natural world, although it was not truly natural.

I, along with my group, had been out on boats among the mangrove backwaters in the south of the island. We had observed some beautiful birdlife. There was an abundance of kingfishers with their exquisite plumage.

Tucked away in a corner of the mangrove there was what looked like a fish farm. It wasn't a fish farm, although it did involve fish. It was a foot pedicure spa! They used to be all the rage in the UK but seemed to have disappeared after there were one or two health scares associated with them, and concerns for the welfare of the fish. In Sri Lanka, there are no such concerns.

There were several tanks floating in the mangrove, each containing fish of varying sizes. One, alarmingly, had half a dozen fish in excess of a foot long. I think I would be counting my toes if I had put my feet in that one.

Instead, I was encouraged to put my feet into the tank with the most fish, all about four inches long. Despite sharing the tank with David and Sandie, the fish seemed to prefer my feet. I have never considered my feet to be ticklish but I found it incredibly so, and could not do either of two things. I couldn't keep my feet in for very long and I could not stop laughing. It was hilarious, and not something I ever want to repeat.

9

STOK KANGRI - TEARS AND TRIUMPH

When the English educational system changed in the early noughties, we could no longer go to Nepal during the optimum spring season. Importance was placed on the exams at the end of the lower sixth so you could not risk jeopardising them by going on expedition during the weeks before the exams. Because Nepal is in the grip of the monsoon season during the English summer holidays, I had to find a new destination to visit. The obvious choice, if we wanted to keep a rather tenuous link to the Himalayas, was Ladakh. The climate was ideal, with dry summers. Not only did it provide some excellent trekking opportunities; it also provided some challenging peaks, most notably Stok Kangri, at 6153m quite a significant challenge.

Our first venture into Ladakh was in 2003 with a large group of students. Angela and I very nearly didn't get there. Three days before departure, Angela was diagnosed with breast cancer. While I was prepared to drop everything, in order to get treatment started, Angela was determined to see the trip through before getting the treatment she needed. It was a wise decision, because nothing could happen for the month after diagnosis. If she went, she would be much fitter, on her return, to face the treatment. If we had stayed at home we would have done nothing but worry. At least in Ladakh we had plenty to take our minds off the situation.

Having spent a couple of days in Delhi, we flew up to Leh and then acclimatised for three days. Leh is 3500m above sea level and is a bit of a shock when you step off the plane into the clear but rarefied air.

There was plenty to do to get acclimatised. Leh is an oasis of green surrounded by a cold, sandy desert and treeless mountains. There is a lot of army activity in the area, because of its proximity to Kashmir and the Pakistan border. Wherever there are soldiers there needs to be some recreation for them. The golf course is one massive bunker with concrete tees and tarmac greens. The golf ball, reputedly, travels much further at altitude. There are some of the highest cricket pitches in the world, again with tarmac strips. Leh also boasts the highest polo ground in the world.

Leh is a peaceful place. It is quiet. The people, predominantly Buddhist, are gentle and kind. It lies on the northern bank of the River Indus, one of the great South Asian rivers. All along the main street, women sit on the pavement, each selling an array of fresh vegetables. In the morning they all sit on one side of the street and change to the other side in the afternoon, following the shade. The sun is hot and burns quickly in the rarefied atmosphere.

Leh is a good place to acclimatise because it is on a fairly steep slope, and, as the hotel is below the main centre of town, it always necessitates a climb when you leave it. The Dragon Hotel, very Tibetan in design and nature, provided good acclimatisation exercise in itself, being on several levels reached only by outside marble staircases.

Dotted at various intervals along the Indus Valley, within easy reach of Leh, are a number of fascinating Buddhist temples, Thiksey, Shey Palace and Phyang to name but a few. The real acclimatisation test is climbing the 500 steep steps up to the modern Shanti Stupa.

If you can do that without stopping, you are ready for Stok Kangri.

All the time you are in Leh you have a dramatic wall of mountains to the south on the other side of the Indus Valley. Standing out above all other peaks is Stok Kangri, our target, which never looks anything less than daunting.

It takes quite some time to reach the mountain via the Markha Valley but there is always plenty to see and to appreciate. In the village of Yuruche, made up of one house, we were invited into the kitchen to learn of their way of life. In front of the house were a few terraces with crops growing. The household was made up of four generations. What made the family arrangement so unusual was the fact that the three sons had all married the same girl. There was not enough land to support three separate families but, if they combined and amalgamated, the land was sufficient. This kind of cohabitation has been happening for centuries as a means of survival in a very harsh and limiting environment. It seemed to work but that kind of existence must have limitations as even these remote communities become more mobile.

In Markha, because we were providing some support to the school and health post, the whole village came out to entertain us in our camp, offering us a fascinating insight into their culture, music and dance.

As we climbed further up the Markha Valley we began to see another impressive peak, Kang Yahtse, which seemed to be drawing me towards it. Sitting on the moraine above camp in Nimaling, a high grassy area inhabited by nomadic herdsmen and their livestock of goats and cattle, I could visualise a route up one ridge, across the summit ridge and down the other side. Just a dream!

We were still several days from our own climb of Stok Kangri. We still had to cross the 5247m Kangmaru La, followed by two days of descent before heading up towards base camp.

It was on the second day of descent that, for me, it all went pear-shaped. We were not long out of camp, passing some impressively phallic rock pillars that took my attention away from the ground beneath my feet. With a cry of pain I rolled my ankle severely and finished up in a heap on the ground. As time passed, the pain was not easing and I kept having bouts of dizziness and nausea. My trek seemed to be over!

After some time dosed with various painkillers and sporting a tight, supportive dressing, I was able to very tentatively hobble down to an area where the ground flattened out. There, waiting for me, was a pony.

The pony ride was quite uncomfortable. The saddle was wooden and, despite having some rugs for padding, I could still feel the hard edges biting into my buttocks and inner thighs. With a Sherpa pulling the rein and another tapping the pony's rump, we were making good progress while the ground was relatively flat. But at the head of the valley I could see a steep rise ahead. This was going to be interesting.

In Ladakh these ponies normally carry a maximum load of 60kg. I was 90kg. As the ground steepened, the pony slowed and needed more and more encouragement. I began to feel sorry for it, and that sorrow turned to guilt as the pony's legs buckled under my weight and collapsed. I couldn't do this anymore. I rolled off and hobbled up the slope. Provided I could put my foot flat on the ground, I could cope reasonably well. But it was rocky. Those ahead of me spent the time moving stones to the sides of the path in order to give me as flat a route as possible.

When the slope plateaued I was given the option to ride again, but I was managing, slowly, and didn't want to cause any more stress to the pony. I managed to get across the plateau, with regular rests to allow the pain to ease, and I even managed some of the steep descent, using my poles for support.

Eventually, I had to give in and climb on the pony again for the last yards into camp, which also involved a river crossing.

Once in camp I lay in my tent exhausted by the effort and the pain. I knew in my heart that this was as close as I was going to get to Stok Kangri. I was going to have to retreat back to Leh for treatment. I still found it upsetting when I heard that the adults had

had a meeting and decided that I must go down. Karinia, one of the doctors on the trip, would come down with me. She had not coped well with the altitude, so it gave her an opportunity to withdraw.

The next morning, with my eyes filled with tears, I hobbled out of camp with Karinia and a Sherpa towards the nearest road. The rest of the group, including Angela, continued towards Stok Kangri.

I was miserable. I hated being apart from the group. They were my reason for being there and without them I lost all motivation. And that mood never really left me. I went to a clinic where my ankle was X-rayed to reveal that there wasn't a break but it was severely sprained. It was taped up with some sticky, elasticated bandage and I was doomed to wait for the group to return in several days.

I had a very miserable night. I could not just sit around and do nothing. But that is exactly what I had to do, with the exception of a couple of outings hobbling to nearby shops. I was a prisoner and my mood was deteriorating with each passing hour.

I heard that there was a festival taking place at Phyang Monastery. That should be a worthwhile spectacle. A taxi took us to the monastery where there was quite a crowd sitting around the main courtyard. While we waited for the festivities to begin, my eyes were drawn towards Stok Kangri. Phyang Monastery gave me the most perfect view of the mountain and it was painful to think that the group was preparing to climb it without me.

Loud horns, cymbals and drums drew my attention away from the mountains and announced the start of what was to prove to be an exceptionally colourful and dramatic show. I could not pretend to know what was going on but the overriding theme seemed to be good overcoming evil. The grotesque masks and heavy, multi-layered and colourful costumes were fantastic.

When it was all over our taxi took us back to Leh and I had the satisfaction of knowing that I had done something worthwhile and interesting with the day, and hadn't just sat around feeling very sorry for myself.

We still had days to fill, but how to fill them? Let's go white-water rafting on the Indus. It can't be that difficult with a knackered ankle. We made all the necessary arrangements for the next day and I was beginning to feel much more positive.

The next morning a taxi took us to the launching point on the river. I wrapped my foot and lower leg in a couple of polythene bags and taped them up in the hope that they would keep the water out. Unfortunately, I couldn't do any of the manual work associated with the start and finish of a rafting trip, so I happily sat back and let others take the strain. When all was ready we embarked on a three- to four-hour journey along the Indus. The rapids were not particularly feisty but the journey did take us through an impressive gorge.

Back at the hotel in the afternoon, I began to give some thought as to what to do next. We had to fill the time and we were rapidly running out of time fillers. I kept looking across at the peak wondering how they were getting on. One group had gone for the summit the day before and another group was up there today. The thought of waiting for a few more days for the group to arrive in Leh was unthinkable. Why don't we go to meet them?

That is what we did. We took a taxi over to the village of Stok and booked ourselves into the only hotel that seemed to be open. We were the only residents and the owner had to quickly find a cook for us as his normal chef was out in the mountains with a group.

The following morning the owner gave us a lift to the top of the village, where the trail up to base camp starts. Carrying very little and using my poles to take the weight off my ankle we set out at a pretty good pace. The path rises quite gently so progress was good.

I was expecting to see, or rather hear, the group at any time, but there was no sign of them and we got higher and higher. The landscape was becoming more barren and the path trickier, with obstacles that I had to manoeuvre around.

We had been climbing for several hours and had reached around the 5000m contour when we saw a very happy bunch coming towards us. Not expecting to meet us, we were almost upon them when they realised who was hobbling towards them.

There was a great deal of handshaking and hugging and it was great to be back with the group. Angela had succeeded where I had failed; she had reached the summit of Stok Kangri: 6153m! She had achieved a height higher than I had ever been. I was so pleased for her. She looked tired but she also looked great. How was I going to live this down? I had to find a peak higher than Stok Kangri and get to the top.

As we sat chatting underneath the steep valley side, stones began to cascade from above. We had to move quickly out from the slope. A flock of blue sheep were running directly above us. What could have spooked them? The only thing it could have been was a snow leopard. We never saw it but we were assured that that is what would be the cause of the sheep scattering like that.

If I had enjoyed the walk up to meet the group, the walk back down was far less pleasant. My ankle was really beginning to hurt and my pace on the way down was much slower than up. Angela stuck with me and talked all the way back to Stok telling me of her adventure.

In Leh I had a T-shirt embroidered for her:

Stok Kangri 6153m
Angela's been higher than me...
... but I still love her!

That achievement did her the world of good. By the time she got home she was much stronger and fitter. Within three days of our return she was in hospital, having surgery, prior to embarking on a course of chemotherapy and then radiotherapy. Her positive approach allied to her recent remarkable achievement got her through. She climbed two massive mountains that year.

Needless to say, the fact that Angela had been higher than me did not sit comfortably, and for the next couple of years, following her recovery, I plotted to climb higher. In 2005 I took a group to make an attempt on Mera Peak, in Nepal, but had to abandon at just below

6000m because of the poor weather conditions and a feeling that I wasn't capable of reaching the summit. In 2006 I returned to Ladakh with a group of students, with a view to climbing the 6250m Mentok Peak. Again, poor weather forced us to abandon. (More about those two expeditions in other chapters.)

It wasn't until 2008 that I managed to equal Angela's achievement when I returned to Stok Kangri with a large group of thirty-six.

We followed the same route to base camp as in 2003, only I managed to get there this time. Severe flooding in 2006 had changed much of the route beyond recognition.

The night before setting out on the climb, we kitted everybody out with crampons and ice axes, although we hoped that their use would be minimal. Thirty-three of us were heading for the summit, the three doctors happy with their achievement of reaching base camp.

The alarm went off at 1.00am. I'm not sure how much sleep I had achieved, being excited by the challenge that lay ahead. Hot soup was served in the mess tent while we organised everybody into groups, each group having seven students, one member of staff and a crew member.

At 2.15 a line of head torches set off up the first hill. The pace was steady and the line was quiet as everybody focused on the task. I was at the front with the group that needed the most support and encouragement. After half an hour we reached the crest of the first hill and rested for a while, looking down on the night lights of Leh far below and across the Indus Valley. Above, the occasional shooting star cast a trail across the night sky.

We continued along a good path towards the glacier. The gradient was much gentler. As we approached advanced base camp the route became rockier and this trend continued as we got closer to the glacier and the debris it caused.

Cara was feeling very uncomfortable, cold and tired. Certainly, as we got closer to the glacier the temperature dropped. She was in tears and begging to return to camp. An escort was arranged, from one of the crew, to take her, first, to advanced base camp, where she could get a hot drink, and then onward to base camp in daylight. By now there was a faint glow in the east and I was looking forward to seeing the wider view of what we were doing.

We could now see the bulk of Stok Kangri looming above the glacier and it looked quite daunting. By now, another girl, Hannah, was feeling very sick but showed grit and determination, insisting on carrying on.

Crossing the glacier was easy. To my left there was a huge chasm created by the ice pulling away from the rock. By the time we reached the other side of the glacier, Hannah had deteriorated and her legs were buckling under her. There was no other option but to send her back to base camp with another member of the crew.

Now the real climbing started. The gradient was much steeper, made up of loose stones and rock. We could see our targets ahead, the initial one being the ridge and beyond that the summit. It was not going to be quick. We would take a couple of dozen steps and then rest for a minute. Every so often we would take a ten-minute break, which we were always ready for. It was an opportunity to take on a little fuel. Standing there during one of the breaks, I knew that I was going to make it to the top, although I also realised it was going to take some time. The target looked tantalisingly close but never seemed to be getting any closer.

There was very little snow on the face but where there was it was fairly treacherous and the crew had to give support.

Eventually we reached our first target, the ridge. The views over the other side towards the Markha Valley were stunning, with fabulous rock formations and ridge after ridge as far as the eye could see.

Now the ultimate goal was clearly visible: the snow-dome of the summit. It looked so close, but, with three rocky outcrops and some snow to negotiate, it was still going to take a while. While on the face, the ridge looked to be at an easier gradient, but, now we were on it, that proved to be a misconception. Despite the gradient, the altitude and the sheer physical exertion, we did seem to be making progress and the first rocky outcrop was negotiated with ease. The second proved more difficult and the crew had to set up a rope for us to use as a handrail. This all added to the time.

Having cleared the second outcrop, we could see the prayer flags that marked the summit. We were going to make it.

The third outcrop also proved difficult and it was decided to take a circuitous route round it to the right, reducing the level of exposure we would have faced on the rock or to the left of it. The prayer flags were only about 50m from this outcrop and it took us at least half an hour to negotiate our way around it.

Fifteen metres from the summit we reached the snow-dome and felt it prudent to wear our crampons, so more time was spent, delaying us from reaching the summit. The group wanted me to be the first but I was having none of that. I have always looked upon myself as the provider, not the taker, of opportunity, so those that were ready all linked hands and we reached the summit together. We charged up the last few steps to collapse in a line, somewhat surprised by the sudden sheer drop down the other side.

Regaining my breath, I sat on the snow and encouraged the others up to the summit. Hugs were coming at me from all directions and the emotion I felt could not be held back. The tears flowed. I was not the only one, fortunately.

When my composure improved I took the opportunity to look around, take some pictures and revel in the achievement. Then someone would say or do something and my composure would slip again. When Neeraj and I hugged was the worst. He was determined to get me to the top and I am so grateful to him.

Once we left the glacier and started the climb, my admiration for Angela rocketed. At no time did she say how hard it had been. Not once did I hear her complain. Now that I am equal to her, I can only admire her more and more. I say "equal". I do believe that there was an extra foot of snow on the summit, so, technically, I have been higher than her!

It had taken us nine and a half hours to reach the summit and we spent an hour on the top. We had had nothing but blue skies ever since we started out on this trek, and now dark clouds were building around some of the nearby summits, producing rumbles of thunder.

Grabbing a piece of rock for my summit collection, we set off on our descent. It was going to be difficult and it was going to take several hours to reach camp. The route down was straight down the steep face we had traversed on our way up to the ridge. This meant a 500m descent down very unstable scree before the angle began to ease.

Some found the descent exhilarating while others approached it nervously. I focused my attention on supporting those who were nervous. The rocks beneath our feet moved readily downwards, either en masse or individually. There were regular shouts of "Below!" as rocks hurtled towards those lower down. At one point the whole area of the mountain where we were started to slide. This had started from above us and began to pick us up as it reached us.

I shouted to those around me, "Roll to the side and escape the slide."

They responded brilliantly and maintained their position on the mountain. It was exhausting, gradually descending, making sure that those around me were safe and coping with the terrain, while looking out constantly, ensuring that those lower down were not going to be hit by rocks hurtling down the slope.

It took about two hours to complete this part of the descent, and when everybody reached a point of safety we enjoyed a well-earned rest. It was already 3.00pm and we had consumed very little food throughout the climb. Suddenly, I felt hungry and took advantage of a half-hour rest to take on some calories. The sunshine was very warm but the clouds continued to gather. The weather was definitely breaking and, soon after we resumed our descent, it started snowing. Spirits were high, though. There was a sense of pride and achievement among the group, particularly when we looked back at the towering lump of Stok Kangri, looking even more daunting in the gathering storm.

We still had some distance to travel back to camp but at least the going was now much easier.

Back in camp that evening, tiredness soon overcame everybody and there was no celebrating into the night. The crew all came into the mess tent and applauded our effort. The two girls who retreated had made a full recovery and sending them back had been the right decision. I made a point of thanking the doctors for keeping us healthy and giving us the best possible chance of success.

But the story does not end there.

Normally, the descent from base camp to the village of Stok is a five-hour relaxed walk. Remember, I had done a fair portion of it with a dodgy ankle five years previously. While we had been at base camp there had been an event in a side valley that had an immediate impact on the main valley we were to walk down. There were rumours filtering through camp about a landslide. We knew none of the detail.

The weather had not improved overnight and those that had set off for the summit in the early hours began to filter back into camp looking dejected and crestfallen. Conditions on Stok Kangri were terrible, with white-out conditions. We had been so lucky with our timing.

Ignorant of what had happened further down the valley, we set off in high spirits, despite the rain that was now falling. We were making good progress. Neeraj had gone ahead to assess the situation regarding the landslide.

What we came across was not a landslide. It was much worse than that. The terminal moraine of a glacier had collapsed, releasing the lake that it had held back. The hot weather of recent weeks had caused more snow and ice to melt than normal and the volume of the lake had increased, putting pressure on the moraine. The night we had been struggling up Stok Kangri, the moraine gave in to the pressure and sent a deluge of rock, soil and water down the valley, picking up anything that got in its way. By the time it reached the Stok Valley it was unstoppable and, gathering speed and momentum, swept all the way down the valley, swishing from side to side. Mudflows spanned the valley, the river changed course and often became many channels. Paths disappeared.

What should have been an easy walk out was going to develop into an epic. The ponies, which were leading the way and, hopefully, forging a route for us to follow, were having a nightmare. They were sinking up to their bellies in mud and then water. Some were far from happy and tried to escape.

The crew were magnificent. We were faced with at least a dozen river crossings and, each time they would set up a rope to help us, they stood waist deep in the rushing muddy water to ensure our safety. A number of us could not stand by and watch them do all the work, so we got involved and took a share of the burden.

We were constantly working against time. The longer we took, the more likely we would be encountering a surge in water levels as the snowmelt from higher up began to have an effect.

The mud was grey and up to our knees. We tried stepping from stone to stone but they were either wobbly or slippery. We could not afford an accident.

It was like this all the way down the valley and the journey was taking time and energy. It was an exciting adventure but, perhaps, something our tired bodies could have done without after the exertions of the previous few days.

We met trekkers struggling up the valley, people who did not have the support that we had. It was going to be a real struggle for them. Where our paths crossed on a river crossing, we helped them, but their progress was so slow that many ran the risk of being stranded when night fell. We tried to advise them but our advice fell mainly on deaf ears as they had long-planned itineraries to work to, itineraries that paid little heed to natural obstacles.

It was 6.30pm when we reached the outskirts of Stok. It had taken us ten hours!

We were truly exhausted. By the time we reached our camp, in the garden of our chief pony man, all we wanted to do was crawl into our sleeping bags. Not until we had enjoyed a celebratory meal, a few drinks and quite a bit of singing and dancing. We had plenty to celebrate.

10
—

MERA PEAK

I am often asked, "What is the hardest trip you have done?" I think the answer has to be Mera Peak for a number of reasons. At 6476m, it was the highest peak I had attempted to climb. Being quite remote, it was a long trek in, it was colder than most treks and it required a greater degree of skill and determination to reach the summit.

We were quite a large group, twenty-three in total, including two mountaineering guides, John Lyle and Al Gilmore, both from Scotland. There were quite a few new people who had not travelled with me before but who had obviously been drawn to the idea of trekking a difficult peak.

We also had another ambition up our sleeve, to get into the *Guinness Book of Records*. Chris, the medic on this trip, was an enthusiastic morris dancer and he came up with the idea of performing a dance on the summit, making it, surely, the highest morris dance in the world. We needed to make two approaches, the first to the Morris Federation for their blessing, and then to Guinness World Records to formally apply to register the record attempt.

The responses we received were less than encouraging. The Morris Federation's reply was short and sweet: "Are you taking the piss?"

Guinness World Records also declined our idea, stating that they no longer do altitude records because people hop on planes to achieve their record. When we suggested it being a land-based record, their reply was, "We are not entering into correspondence on this matter!" Our hopes were dashed, but we were still going to do it when were reached the summit.

When we arrived in Kathmandu it was as busy as ever, as we had landed in the middle of Holi Festival, where brightly coloured tikka powders and water are thrown in equal measure at anybody who happens to come into the line of fire. Many position themselves on the rooftops to bombard from above. There is no escape.

Having enjoyed Kathmandu, we flew up to Lukla for the start of the long approach to Mera Peak. It had been an early start with the inevitable delay in leaving Kathmandu, while cloud conditions improved in the mountains. By the time we left Lukla half the day had gone. It was a harsh introduction to the trek, with a 600m descent followed by a long 600m ascent. Bizarrely, we were heading south, away from the mountains, but it was the only sensible way to get to Mera Peak. From Lukla there are two ways to approach the mountain, either over the Zawtra La or the longer route over the Pangkongma La into the Hinku Valley. If you take the former, the ascent is immediately much too great and you stand a greater chance of failure. It is much better to follow the much longer and gradual second option.

Needless to say, neither option was easy, and the days were long and hard. We just hoped that by the time we reached the mountain we would be fit enough for the long grind to the summit.

In order to get into the Hinku Valley we had to cross a number of ridges, the last, Pangkongma La being the highest and fully covered with deep snow. We used it as a means of practising our use of crampons before we dropped again below the snow line.

The Hinku Valley is very remote so it has no permanent settlements. A few farmers go up there during the warmer months to graze their flocks and there are a few teahouses, catering for trekkers on their way to Mera Peak. Mera is quite popular as it is the highest peak you can climb that is not technical or very exposed. Assuming the weather is in your favour, you are fit and you can cope with the altitude, you should be able to reach the summit.

Once in the Hinku Valley you appreciate the remoteness and the wild nature of the valley. A rippling scar runs the full length where the earth has been scoured and all vegetation plucked and carried down valley.

In early September 1998, a large section of hanging glacier collapsed into Sabai Tsho Lake at the head of the valley. The shock exerted enormous pressure on the terminal moraine holding the lake, so much so that it collapsed, allowing water, rocks and ice to cascade, scouring the floor and lower sides of the valley. This one episode caused the level of the lake to drop 50m. Two houses were destroyed and three yaks killed, which goes to highlight the isolation of the valley.

By the time we reached Tangnag we were back into fresh snow, although it often went as quickly as it came, the sun evaporating it rather than melting it. We took time to visit Sabai Tsho Lake. We approached it through the gaping channel created by the collapse of the moraine. The original water line was clearly visible. The surface of the lake was slush, on the verge of freezing, but not quite. When we threw a stone into the water the ripples froze.

The severity of the trek was beginning to tell and Judith was suffering from altitude sickness. The only way out from this situation involved going even higher, back the way we had come or over the Zawtra La, unless we ordered a helicopter. Chris, our doctor for the trip, decided she needed to be evacuated, so a helicopter was requested.

At the same time, we met three students from Cardiff University on their way down. They were suffering from frostbite, not having worn appropriate footwear for their summit bid. It was decided to evacuate them as well.

While Chris was managing all this, the rest of us continued up to

Khare, where we were to set up base camp. It was also an opportunity to acclimatise further to the altitude, before the climb.

Khare is a small hamlet of three or four houses nestling at the foot of the lateral moraine of the Mera Glacier. It was a cold and miserable place in the most incredible of surroundings. High snow and rock peaks were all around us.

By now we had all developed high-altitude coughs, the result of breathing in cold air through our mouths. I had coughed so much that I had torn all the intercostal muscles on the left side of my ribs. Coughing was agony, as was laughing, sneezing, breathing and talking. One of the group, Mark, a surgeon, wanted to operate with his Swiss army knife to relieve some of the pressure, but I was not willing to let him loose on me.

We acclimatised by visiting a side valley, at the head of which was a perfect pyramidal peak. This exploration gave Chris time to catch up with us, having dealt safely with the various casualties.

Some of the group decided that Khare was as far as they wanted to go and chose to stay there when the rest of us set off for the summit.

The next day we set off for high camp at about 5800m. This took us up the lateral moraine to the Mera La, where we kitted up for travelling up the glacier. This involved harnesses, ropes, ice axes and crampons. We were working in groups of four or five, each group with a Sherpa in the lead, and had about 4m of rope between each of us. Now that we joined the glacier we headed straight up it towards the summit. We were exposed to extremely high winds, which gusted across the ice.

Every time a gust hit us we had to crouch down on the ice to stop ourselves from being blown over. Every so often there were crevasses to step over. None of them was particularly wide but we were grateful that we were all linked together just in case. If one did fall down a crevasse, there would be enough weight on the rope to arrest the fall and prevent injury.

The going was slow. Every breath hurt. We would take ten steps and then rest for a minute before taking another ten steps. We were concentrating so much on our breathing, counting steps and ducking whenever a gust of wind hit us, that we did not really take time to appreciate the beauty of our surroundings. It was a lot of trouble to take gloves off in order to fiddle with the camera to take pictures. All the time the gloves were off the fingers got colder and colder and more painful. Nevertheless, I did get a picture as we rested on the ice and it was worth the cold fingers. Wow!

We reached high camp, a rocky outcrop above the glacier. The crew had arrived the day before to set up the mess tent and our tents, all weighted down with rocks, as pegs were no use in this environment. It was bitterly cold so the only thing we could do was climb into our sleeping bags and hope that we warmed up.

The Sherpas brought us bowls of hot, steaming noodle soup, full of goodness and energy. Chris was struggling. He had not had the benefit of acclimatising at Khare and was feeling very cold. There were three to a tent so, hopefully, we would generate some heat and warm each other up.

As soon as the soup was consumed, we settled down for the night, anticipating an early start for the summit. Sleep was very difficult. Not only was it very cold but the wind was fierce, noisily buffeting the tents. Chris was shivering, so I spent the night with my arms wrapped around him in an effort to warm him up.

At one point we heard shouts from one of the other tents but could not make out what they were saying. They were having some difficulty, but nobody really wanted to leave their sleeping bag to help. It was very mean of us. We discovered in the morning that the wind had broken their tent poles and they spent the night holding the tent up with their walking poles.

Our tent also suffered, the wind pulling at the flysheet, whipping it off so we only had a single shell protecting us. Throughout the night we were sprinkled with little shards of ice as our breath froze on the canvas and then fell onto us. It has to be one of the most uncomfortable nights I have ever experienced, so much so that, when the time came to kit up for the summit, I just did not have the energy or the will, despite the fact that the morning was perfect. The wind had dropped, there was not a cloud in the sky and everything looked perfect. I was happy, sitting in the sun, trying to absorb any warmth I could and watching others head for the summit. Even the thought of exceeding the height Angela had climbed in 2003 was no incentive. I was not alone. A number of us had decided that enough was enough; we had reached our limit on this occasion.

It was not long before those who had set out for the summit were returning. The wind and snow had hidden all the crevasses, which were much wider higher up, and it was decided that it was too dangerous to continue. They got to within about 300 vertical metres of the summit.

Before leaving camp, we had more hot soup and carrying our own thoughts, we headed back down the glacier to Khare. With each step down I began to feel better, both physically and mentally. It still hurt to breathe. Yes, I was disappointed about not having it in me to reach the summit, but I have always said, "It is not the summit that matters, but the journey." It is so true.

Normally, the walk out is easy, and so it was, as we descended the Hinku Valley. The sting in the tail was the Zawtra La. It was a long, very steep climb up towards the pass and by the time we reached it we were walking in deep snow. There is a section at the top of the pass that traverses the slope. The snow-laden path is on a slight slope with a long drop to the left, making us feel exposed in such conditions. We should really have put our crampons on. As we looked down from the second summit of the Zawtra La, we realised the need for them. The route down was very steep through deep snow, requiring not only crampons but a rope and the use of Prusik loops, a system by which you can make a controlled descent.

It was here, more than anywhere, that we had concern for the welfare of our porters, who were carrying huge loads with nothing more than plimsolls on their feet. They did have two-point instep crampons to wear. I think our concern arose, largely, because we had three young lady porters, whom we thought might have difficulty with the snow and steepness of the slope, a section that was in the region of 100m long, far enough to hurt yourself if you fell.

We need not have worried. Our high-spirited porters donned their instep crampons, and, smiling and laughing, dropped down from the summit and danced down the slope. We, despite having all the protective gear, approached the descent gingerly. At one point I was waist deep in snow with one foot stuck between two rocks while the other was splayed across the surface of the snow. I struggled to find the leverage to extricate the one foot without digging myself deeper into the snow. All the time the effort was causing pain in my ribs. Eventually rescue came and dug me out of my predicament.

Once we were out of the snow the descent became less steep and easier. Just one more camp before we reached Lukla, where we tried to create a mountain out of empty beer cans.

We may not have reached the summit of Mera Peak; it may have been a physically and mentally challenging trek but it was also most enjoyable. We did consider returning another year to see if we could, to put it in the words of Ed Hillary, "Knock the bastard off!" We decided not to, in the end, as the outcome might be the same and that would have really dented our pride.

We never did get the chance to do our morris dance on the summit.

11

—

THE JOY OF PERU

My thirst for travel and for new cultures led me to other parts of the world. I still loved the Himalayas and all that they offer, but I wanted to broaden my horizon to include other great mountain ranges. They don't come much greater than the Andes, the backbone of the South American continent. I also wanted to provide variety for those who travel with me.

My first venture into South America, with a group of sixth-formers, took me to Peru. It seemed the perfect destination. It had everything – a Pacific coastline, superbly sculptured mountains, rainforest, a fascinating history and much, much more. We were relying on a company, Explorandes, who had won numerous ecotourism awards, to be our hosts and to provide us with a trip of a lifetime.

Peru maintains that its tourist industry benefits most when Nepal faces difficulty. The Maoist insurgency in Nepal from 1996 to 2006 put many people off travelling there. Similarly, the earthquake of 2015 caused more people to consider Peru as a safer option. Of course, Peru, too, has had its difficulties, with the Shining Path Movement of the 1980s and '90s. The fact that Peru has experienced political stability in recent decades is enough to encourage tourism.

Unfortunately, Peru is a long way from the UK and flights can be expensive, particularly when compared with flights to Nepal. The distance was apparent when I first travelled there in 2007. It takes a long time to cross the Atlantic, and as long again to cross the Amazon Rainforest. In fact, we were only half an hour from our landing in Lima and we were still over the rainforest with not an Andean mountain in sight. Then, suddenly, we were flying over snow-capped mountain peaks, but no sooner had we spotted them then they were behind us and we were descending towards Lima over the grey, cloudy Pacific Ocean.

The cold Humboldt Current, travelling north from the Antarctic, affects the Peruvian coast. For six months of the year the coast is shrouded in mist, rolling in off the ocean. In Lima, they may not see the sun for six months. We were only there for a short time but it still had an effect. It cast a gloom over Lima that left us disappointed. I am sure Lima can be very pleasant but we did not see it at its best. Unfortunately, it was not much better when I revisited the city in 2009 with another group, although I was prepared for the grey light cast over us.

On each of my visits, the journey out of Lima was the same. We headed north along the Pacific Highway for 200km, then went inland towards the mountains. The damp air followed us all the way up the coast. You would have thought that all this moisture would have encouraged vegetation, but there was very little, and, most often, none. The journey was punctuated with police checks. They were not interested in us as passengers but in finding some small fault with the driver's paperwork or with the vehicle itself. Money would change hands and we would be waved on our way. Lunch money!

As soon as we headed inland and began to climb, we left the coastal cloud behind us and emerged into glorious sunshine. We stopped for lunch in a small village square with a number of stalls selling fruit and vegetables at the roadside. I was fascinated by both the quality of produce on offer and the way it was displayed. I was looking for something I had not seen before and came across a fruit about the size of a large apple, but with an un-apple-like appearance. It was cherimoya. It was wonderful, tasting of apple and custard. On several occasions, I bought some to share with the group.

We continued to climb, passing acres and acres of red chillies drying in the sunshine. Women, in large hats, sat among them, sorting and turning them in order to get the full benefit of the piercing sunshine.

In a few hours we climbed from sea level to 4000m. When we jumped out of the vehicle at the high point to admire the views across to the Cordillera Huayhuash (pronounced whywash), we suddenly realised that we could not rush about without feeling breathless and light-headed.

After a long journey, we reached Huaraz, a town where we were to acclimatise for a couple of days. At 3000m above sea level, it is ideal.

Architecturally, Huaraz has nothing going for it. It is a modern city of low-rise buildings built on a grid system of roads. The city's lack of beauty is more than compensated for by the surrounding mountains. To the north is the Cordillera Blanca, with Huascaran, Peru's highest mountain, dominating the skyline. Other, less lofty mountains surround the city.

There is a reason why Huaraz does not have any of the historical charm that other Peruvian cities have. In May 1970, a devastating earthquake struck the region, flattening the city. Seventy thousand people were killed, with another 50,000 injured.

Some years before the earthquake, there was a lawyer in the town of Yungay, a few miles north of Huaraz. Although a married man, he was having an affair with his secretary. All was going well until the secretary fell pregnant. This would prove very problematical for him, so he murdered the secretary, dismembered her body, put it into bags and threw the bags into the Rio Santa, the river that flowed through the town. Unfortunately, for him, the bags caught on rocks, the body was discovered, and the lawyer arrested. He was found guilty and sent to prison for twelve years.

The damaged building at Khumjung School

Meeting Ed Hillary and George Lowe in Kathmandu

King's Peak (Nobby's View) with Cho Oyu behind

View from King's Peak with Everest far left of picture

An agitated male Orang-utan in Sumatra

The flicking tongue of a Komodo dragon

White rhino in Chitwan National Park, Nepal

Ticklish feet in Sri Lanka

Looking across to Stok Kangri from Phyang in 2003

Taking a break during the climb of Stok Kangri in 2008

Celebrating the ascent of Stok Kangri (6153m), on the summit in 2008

Preparing to climb the glacier on Mera Peak

High camp on platform overlooking the Mera Glacier

Mera Peak 6476m – so close, yet so far!

Morning reflection, Carhuacocha

Glacial lake with Jirishanca behind

Descending from the San Antonio Pass

While the boys got on with labouring in the school, the girls learnt a variety of craft techniques

Machu Picchu

Jancapampa mushroom hat child

Cusco Cathedral

Welcome party on the Islas Uros

The crashed lorry that caused the loss of the passport

Druk White Lotus School, Ladakh, 12 hours before it was engulfed in mud, rocks and water

Share the Vision: top row from top left – guiding in the Jebel Sahro, Morocco, elephant bathing in Nepal, guiding in the Sahara Desert.
Bottom row – Iceland, guiding and white water rafting

Potala Palace, Lhasa, Tibet

Debating monks at Sera Monastery

Everest from the Rongbuk Monastery, Tibet

Children of the Tibetan plateau

Trekking north side of Everest   *A camp and breakfast with a view!*

Scenes from the north side of K2

The author with the children of Kangchenjunga Basic School, Taplejung, NE Nepal

Morning 'Brain Gym' at the start of the day

Pupils of Sundevi Secondary School, Taplejung

Destroyed classrooms after the 2015 earthquake

New classrooms built following the earthquake

All children now have a midday meal

Children are always very eager to learn

Upon his release, he decided to celebrate with his whole family, who descended upon Yungay for the happy event. The party took place on 31 May 1970. Immediately above the town is the towering bulk of Huascaran North. The earthquake caused the mountain to split and a mass of rock, ice and snow came cascading down the slopes to completely engulf the town, killing the lawyer and all of his close and extended family. This event was referred to as the secretary's revenge!

The only survivors in the town of Yungay that day were the audience attending a circus just outside the town and a school group visiting a cemetery. The cemetery was built in tiers, and, remarkably, all the children were on the top tier, watching the lower tiers being consumed by the debris.

After a number of days exploring the surroundings, including some turquoise mountain lakes, acclimatising and preparing our bodies for high-altitude trekking, we headed off for our treks. In 2007, with the students, we headed south to the Cordillera Huayhuash, which we were going to circumnavigate, while in 2009 we headed north to trek the Santa Cruz section of the Cordillera Blanca.

Our crew, on each occasion was made up of some very interesting characters. Miguel was our guide. He spoke excellent English, having spent some time in the USA. His knowledge of all aspects of the environment was superb. But, I understood, he relied heavily on his support team for their knowledge of the areas we were trekking. In the Huayhuash, we had Guicho, who was well into his seventies. Dressed in his pressed trousers, jacket and trilby hat, he cut a fine figure. Despite his age, his pace never changed, whether climbing steeply or descending. He had spent most of his life in these mountains as a cattle rustler, so knew them intimately. He was a real character. Angel was another aging stalwart of the team.

In the Cordillera Blanca, Miguel relied heavily on two more similarly clad gentlemen, in their seventies, leading the way. Their knowledge of the mountains was brought about by years of checking the stability of terminal moraines holding back glacial lakes.

We had one further companion on each of our trips. A small stuffed bear going by the name of Paddington. We decided to take Paddington home. Miguel had no knowledge of Paddington but was fascinated by the story surrounding him. Paddington came everywhere with us and had some wonderful adventures, even having a go at horse riding. Naturally, we left him in the good care of Miguel when we left and I learnt some time after my return home that Paddington had made an appearance on Peruvian radio and TV.

The mountains of the Cordillera Huayhuash are all stunningly beautiful and, because the chain of the Andes is very narrow, we were able to see them from every angle. With names like Rondoy, Jirishanca, Yerupajá (the highest peak), Siula Grande and Sarapo, and with glacier encrusted, rocky faces leading to pinnacle summits, they provide some of the best views in the world. Beneath all this beauty are pristine lakes of turquoise blue glacial melt water.

What makes the mountains so beautiful is that you are able to get very close to them. They are not bulky, wide-based mountains, but rise steeply on all sides. They are not as high as the Himalayas, ranging between 5500m and 6500m, so it is possible to get closer. That closeness allowed us to see every detail of the mountains, from the variations in rock to the intricate patterns of the snow flutings clinging to their near vertical surfaces. I never got tired of just gazing at them and watching their features change with the light. All these factors make these mountains some of the most stunning in the world.

At the time of our visit in 2009 there had been a poll to see which was the most beautiful mountain in the world. It was no surprise that, in the top three, the Matterhorn and Ama Dablam were placed, but so was Alpamayo, at No. 1. You could put those three in any order you like and still have, perhaps, the most magnificent peaks in the world.

The Huayhuash range is compact. This is clear when you consider that it is only about 30km long by 15km wide. In order to traverse it we had to cross nine high-altitude passes, each one revealing more superb views.

The most dramatic was the San Antonio Pass, at 5000m, one of the highest. From the top we looked down steeply towards more of those lovely lakes and a wall of snow-fluted mountains.

From our camp at the base of the pass, we travelled up a side valley to look down on the glacier and across to the peaks of Sarapo and Siula Grande. From our vantage point we were able to look out to where the most dramatic mountain story, Joe Simpson's *Touching the Void*, happened. We were able to look across to the summit ridge where Joe had his accident and broke his leg. We could see the line of descent that he made with Simon Yates lowering him down the face of the mountain. We could see the glacier, into which Joe fell when Simon realised that his own survival depended on him cutting the rope. We couldn't see the icy tomb into which Joe fell but we could see the jumble of ice and rock that he had to crawl along for five miles in order to reach safety. Looking at the scene it seemed remarkable that he survived, and that he had the determination to do so.

We had some amazing campsites. The one that stands out more than the others is the one at Carhuacocha, on the lakeside with a wall of majestic peaks on the far shore. The east-facing wall was aglow with orange light reflected in the water in the morning.

We were camping here for two nights to give us a chance to acclimatise, to visit other lakes, even closer to the mountains, and for Robbo, one of my staff colleagues, to go fishing. We had heard that there were trout in the lake and he just happened to have a lightweight telescopic fishing rod with him. He took himself off for a bit of solitary fishing. He failed to get a bite. We did have trout for dinner that night, caught by the crew using the Peruvian method. They don't bother with the lake but fish in one of the pools in the outflow stream. They place their net across the bottom end of the pool and throw soil into the water at the top end. This alarms the fish and they dart to get away from the debris being thrown into their pool, straight into the net. Robbo's hook did come in useful when the crew lost their net in the bottom of the pool. He was able to retrieve it for them.

And now for a sad tale. Just as in Nepal, trekking groups in Peru attract stray dogs. In 2007 we had a puppy join us and we named him Hilario. He was a beautiful puppy and had a wonderful nature, endearing himself to everybody, trekkers and crew alike. At the end of the trek we were worried what was to happen to Hilario. None of us liked the idea of abandoning him when we climbed aboard our bus. Fortunately, one of the kitchen crew offered to give him a home and bring him up as a pet.

When I enquired about the wellbeing of Hilario in 2009, I was saddened to learn that he had been killed. Thieves broke into his new owner's house and poisoned him!

The circuit of the Santa Cruz section of the Cordillera Blanca in 2009 was equally demanding and spectacular, drawing us as close to the mountains as possible. The area around Alpamayo was particularly stunning.

This trek, though, was different. It gave us more contact with local people. Having trekked over the 4400m Putaputa Pass to access the valley of Jancapampa, we came across a group of people that are unique. They wear mushroom felt hats, unlike any hats worn in the rest of Peru. First the children came into camp and sat watching our every movement. If we disappeared into our tents, they would lie down with an eye close to the ground in the hope that they could still watch us through the gap between flysheet and the earth.

The next morning all the women came into camp and sat patiently waiting for something to happen. We decided that this was probably going to be our closest contact with mountain people, so gave them our goodie bags containing knitted teddies, little toys, pencils and crayons, toothpaste and brushes and a whole range of other small items. They were so pleased to be given these items and were very gracious in their acceptance of gifts. They were a delightful community.

Apart from the Kangchenjunga Trek in 2001, I have always tried to make sure that I have a doctor with us, somebody with far greater knowledge than a mountain first aid certificate provides. We had an incident on the Santa Cruz trek that made me very grateful for medical expertise.

We were a couple of hundred metres from camp. Most of the group had already reached camp, but I was bringing up the rear with three others. There was a small stream to cross. Unfortunately, the bridge had collapsed and it was a delicate manoeuvre to get across the broken timbers without slipping into the stream.

One of the three, Tony, jokingly said, "I'll go before you, John. You might break it further."

With that, he lightly skipped across, but, in doing so, slipped and had to lunge for the far bank.

On the far side was the old concrete foundation for the bridge with steel reinforcing rods sticking up out of it. Tony's face and the reinforcing rod came into contact! It cut through his cheek, and because there was a bend in the end of the rod, it hit the back of his throat. Those who saw it all winced. Tony drew his face away from the rod. There was a mark where the rod had been but no noticeable hole. There was also very little blood.

Magda, the doctor, having been summoned, came to see him. Without fuss, she applied some Steri-Strips and walked a slightly shocked Tony into camp. Tony was incredibly lucky. Yes, his cheek had been pierced, but that rod could have taken an eye out or severed an artery. His throat was sore for a couple of days, making swallowing difficult. His cheek healed without leaving a scar.

On the last night of both treks we enjoyed a pachamanca, an Inca-style meal. It was fascinating watching the crew prepare the ingredients. First, they dig a pit in the ground. Around it they build a dome of granite rocks with a small opening on one side. Into that they put pieces of wood and set it alight, regularly introducing more wood to the fire. After a couple of hours, the stones are extremely hot.

Next they scrape out the embers of the fire before collapsing the dome into the pit. In among the stones they place the meat, which has been pre-wrapped in foil. The meat for us was lamb and chicken.

On top of the meat they placed potatoes, both normal and sweet potatoes.

During the course of the preparation they had cut some reeds from the lakeshore, which they now place over the whole area. In among the reeds they sprinkled broad beans and covered it all with a tarpaulin, and shovelled the soil from making the pit, over the top.

After about forty minutes, they started to dismantle the layers, retrieving the food as they did so. It was served up and, goodness, what a feast it was!

The cook boys take a great deal of pride in their work, dressing in white kitchen outfits, including chef's hats, before every meal. The standard of hygiene is excellent. For handwashing, they hang an upturned old coke bottle full of hot water. To wash your hands, you simply loosen the cap so that a trickle of hot water comes out. This way, no water is wasted.

After the trek we returned to Lima for just one night. Remarkably, on both occasions the cloud had lifted and the sun shone down on the city. Immediately, it seemed more lively and vibrant, with so much going on in the streets around Miraflores, the upmarket end of town.

From there we took an early morning flight to Cusco, a city steeped in Inca and colonial history. At an altitude of almost 3500m it is a city to be enjoyed at leisure. It is a beautiful city. What Huaraz would have been if the earthquake had not occurred. Old buildings with pantiled roofs, cobbled streets with arcaded shops and restaurants providing shade from the heat of the sun, wide squares that just lend themselves to people watching. There's a mixture of baroque Spanish convents and monasteries, including the Cathedral Basilica of the Assumption of the Virgin, located on the Plaza de Armas, sitting side by side with ancient Incan temples. The artwork in the cathedral is interesting. It appears to be in the style of the European Renaissance artists but the paintings have innocence and a simplicity about them that confirms they are the work of Quechan artists who have been taught the style. The most interesting picture is that of the last supper, where, on a platter, lies a guinea pig!

The Convent of Santo Domingo, in Cusco, is built on the site of Qorikancha, destroyed during the Spanish invasion. They could not completely destroy it and chose to use some of the foundation stones for the convent. Parts of the original Inca temple have been reconstructed.

Around Cusco there are a number of Inca sites, the most impressive being the fortress known as Sacsayhuamán (pronounced sexy-hu-men). Although a ruin, it is impossible not to marvel at the craftsmanship and engineering that went into its construction. All the stones are cut geometrically and fit together without the need for any binding compound. The sheer size of some of the stones beggars belief as to how they were moved. There are some, particularly corner stones, that are 4m high and 1m square. Sacsayhuamán also gives you an excellent panoramic view of Cusco.

In 2007 the students took some time out to visit the small village of Soqma, en route to Machu Picchu. The journey had been following the Urubamba River, but in order to reach Soqma we had to take a detour into a hanging valley above the main valley.

Camp was on the school playground, which was convenient as we were working in the school, not in a teaching capacity but in creating a new classroom from an existing building. The community had already done the bulk of the work, putting on a new roof and fitting new windows. When we arrived there was already a gang of men working on digging up the solid earth floor with pickaxes. It needed to be lowered by 15cm so that a layer of hardcore could be put down to give a stable base for a concrete floor.

There were too many in the group to all work on the classroom. Although it seemed sexist, the boys joined the men in the classroom, while the girls joined the women of the village, to help prepare a meal for us all.

It was still crowded in the classroom and potentially quite dangerous, with pickaxes and shovels swinging freely and not a hard hat in sight. There were lumps of rock in the mud floor, which either needed digging out or breaking up. Either way, it was pretty physical work. Despite the language barrier, a good bond was being created between the two teams and, although we were all working well together, there was still plenty more to do by the end of the day.

The girls, too, were having a good time, learning a great deal about catering in very basic kitchens. I took some time out to join them. They, too, seemed to be developing a bond with the women of the village. The women were surprised that we knew how to peel and chop potatoes! In front of the wood stove a line of guinea pigs were roasting on spits. We were honoured guests.

That evening, we all crowded into one of the classrooms for our feast, including guinea pig. It tasted very like chicken but there was not a great deal of meat to be had from each animal. The meal was accompanied by a lot of smiling faces and laughter. It seemed the villagers enjoyed having us visit them, as much as we were enjoying the experience. During the conversation, we learnt that we were the first group of tourists to visit the village and offer support.

Before we started work the next day, we gathered all the items we had brought to give away on the playground. We created two piles, one for the school and another to give to each of the children. The children watched in anticipation but they were going to have to wait until later in the day.

While the children went to class, we went back to work, digging out more of the floor before putting down a layer of hardcore, ensuring it was as level as possible. This job was to take us all day.

The girls, in the meantime, spent the day learning crafts from the women of the village. They each made a doll dressed in Quecha costume, learnt how to spin wool, the skill of wool winding and wool dying, using natural colouring.

After lunch, before we went back to our work, we distributed all the gifts we had brought for the village. The children were very excited. The adults, too, appreciated our gesture.

As we finished work on the classroom an Andean priest arrived to perform a special ceremony in our honour, while the village men turned their hand to making a pachamanca for us. Another delicious meal.

The next morning, our last in the village, we just had one more job to do in the classroom, and the girls could join in as well. Before the floor was cemented, we needed to plaster the walls. That may sound quite grand and technical for a group of seventeen-year-olds, but that was not the case. Plastering, Peruvian style, requires a tin bath of liquid plaster, a sheep's fleece and a willingness to get involved, come what may. The sheep's fleece was cut into pieces about twice the size of a hand, which we then dipped into the liquid plaster before slapping it against the wall. Needless to say, it went everywhere! Before long, the potential for some fun was seen, and soon people were slapping each other with the fleece as well as the wall. There was a lot of good-hearted messy fun.

Unbelievably, the task was completed, but everybody was plastered from head to foot with the quickly drying plaster. There really wasn't anywhere in the village where we could wash, but we were told of a waterfall we could use further up the valley. It took a while to get there and by then the plaster was well and truly set on our clothes and skin.

The washing facility was a narrow, 200m waterfall of icy-cold water that hurt as it hit the body, particularly a head like mine with no hair to protect it. The water eventually softened the plaster stuck to skin but, despite its force, the water did little to remove the plaster from clothing.

By the time we returned to the village, they had set up some speakers and a sound system to the battery of a lorry, and we had a final, farewell party with the villagers, dancing and singing. As we left we had to walk down a tunnel of friends, who all wanted to shake hands or embrace us. We had only been there a few days but the strength of the relationship we created, in such a short time, was very strong.

There are a number of ways of approaching Machu Picchu. The train takes you into the village of Aguas Calientes. There, regular buses take you up the winding road to the main entrance. If you have never seen Machu Picchu before, this is a fantastic way to visit. We followed this route in 2007 after leaving Soqma. It was late in the day and we were able to return the following morning for sunrise.

In 2009, we took the train as before, but got off at kilometre 106, a few kilometres short of Aguas Calientes. We were due to get off at kilometre 104 but there had been a fire on the Inca Trail and the path was closed. At the side of the railway track there was a path heading up steeply through trees, normally used by porters. It continued to rise steeply for some time as we climbed high above the Urubamba River, eventually emerging onto the Inca Trail and the terraced ruins of Winayhuayna. These ruins are superb, all the more so because we didn't have to share them with any other people. It gave us a taste of what was to come.

Having recovered from the climb and absorbed the atmosphere of Winayhuayna, we followed the Inca Trail towards Machu Picchu. This took us to the Sun Gate, and, having taken the bus from Aguas Calientes on my previous visit, the Sun Gate is by far the best way to first feast your eyes on Machu Picchu. It is just an incredible sight, looking down upon the ancient city, still a further half an hour's walk away.

We sat on the stone terracing and just stared in awe at the sight. One of our guides, it turned out, was a professional musician, and, as we took in the scene, he played traditional Peruvian music on his pipe. We were so lucky.

As in 2007, we spent two days exploring Machu Picchu, some climbing to the top of the towering Huayna Picchu, the rock tower at the far end of the settlement, while others visited the Inca Bridge, a bamboo bridge clinging to a sheer rock face with no protection. You cannot spend enough time here, although it is best either very early or late in the day, when there are fewer people.

Leave we had to, either to return home, as we did in 2007, or to visit Lake Titicaca, as we did in 2009.

Lake Titicaca is a huge body of water and, at 3800m, is the world's highest navigable lake.

During our journey and in the town of Puno, on the lakeshore, we had seen many women wearing bowler hats. Surely these are not traditional Peruvian hats? They may not have been to begin with but they certainly are now. In the pioneering railway days, many of the engineers came out from the UK to help with the laying of track. They all wore bowler hats. The Peruvian women liked the style and adopted it for themselves.

The main attraction of Lake Titicaca, apart from the crystal-clear waters reflecting the blue sky, are the Islas Uros, man-made reed islands that are home to Uros communities that live permanently on the lake.

They have created a series of floating reed islands. Each island is home to a number of families who, to a large extent today, earn their living from fishing and selling crafted goods to tourists.

As we approached the first island, a reception of rotund, bowler-hatted, vividly dressed women were there to meet us. We had an eye-opening time there. They made us feel very welcome and we learnt a lot about their chosen lifestyle.

The islands are made up entirely of the totora reed that grows abundantly around the shores of the lake. There are several layers to the construction and each island is anchored to the lakebed. Each island is a community in itself but, if there happens to be one family that does not fit in and do their fair share of the community work, the other families cut them off and set them adrift.

All the buildings on the islands are made of reeds. Also their boats, long canoes, are made of reeds, although modern ideas have been introduced into their construction. Reeds eventually rot, and when they do so the canoe is no longer of use. There are a lot of reeds involved in the construction, and, because they spend all their time in the water, their lifespan is limited. Now, they have been innovative in the construction. Instead of having reed boats, they collect plastic bottles from Puno and fit them all together to create two floatation chambers. They then create an outer skin of reeds, which means that they always have a buoyant canoe and they only have to change the outer skin when its condition deteriorates.

We spent a fascinating few hours with these communities, who maintain their ancestral traditions with little modern and environmental intervention.

Sadly, I have not been back to Peru since 2009. If you were to ask me, "Which is the best country you have been to?" it would be very hard not to put Peru at the top of the list, and that is without visiting all those other incredible Andean countries just begging to be visited.

12

CLIMATE CHANGE

One of the reasons for choosing Ladakh as an adventure destination was because it was reputed to have a very stable climate. It is really a high-altitude desert in the rain shadow created by the Himalayan ranges further south, so, while the monsoon rains restrict activities in the Nepal and Indian Himalayas, Ladakh's weather is predictably dry. I don't recall having to wear waterproofs at all during my first trip in 2003. The same cannot be said for subsequent trips. We found ourselves in some fairly dangerous situations as a result of weather.

Looking at the chart on page 92, you would think that organising an expedition in July and August would be a fairly safe option, despite that being the wettest time of the year. The amounts of rain are negligible. The weather and events that we experienced in 2006 and 2010, perhaps, suggest that climate change was occurring.

In 2006 I decided to organise a trek in the Spiti Valley, starting in Kibber and ending up at Lake Tsomoriri.

It was a long journey. The first leg involved taking the train from Delhi to Chandigarh. The railway announcements at Delhi station entertained us as we awaited our train. Each announcement

Average temperatures and precipitation in Leh-Ladakh
(3500 metres altitude)

Month	Max/Min (°C)	Max/Min (°F)	Precipitation	Rain days
January	−3/−15	27/5	9mm (0.4in)	1.3 days
February	−1/−12	30/10	8mm (0.3in)	1.1 days
March	6/−6	43/21	11mm (0.4in)	1.3 days
April	12/−1	54/30	9mm (0.4in)	1.0 days
May	17/3	63/37	9mm (0.4in)	1.1 days
June	21/7	70/45	4mm (0.2in)	0.4 days
July	25/10	77/50	15mm (0.6in)	2.1 days
August	24/9	75/48	15mm (0.6in)	1.9 days
September	21/5	70/41	9mm (0.4in)	1.2 days
October	14/−1	57/30	8mm (0.3in)	0.4 days
November	7/−7	45/19	4mm (0.2in)	0.5 days
December	1/−11	34/12	5mm (0.2in)	0.7 days

was preceded with a chord being played on an organ, followed by, "May I have your attention, please?" This would be followed by an explanation regarding a minor delay in the arrival of a train from the other side of the country. "I regret to inform you that the 08.33 from Kolkata is running two minutes late." All announcements would end with "The inconvenience is deeply regretted" and concluded with another blast of the chord. You could not help but believe in their sincerity. What is more, you had to admire the clarity of the announcement. Every word was enunciated clearly and could be heard over any other noises on the station.

From Chandigarh, vehicles took us up to the hill town of Shimla, the seat of British rule in India during the hot summer months. Shimla, like Darjeeling in the east, is a very British town with very English-looking churches, hotels in colonial buildings with manicured gardens and the Gaiety Theatre, which would look just as at home in an English county town. Tall trees cast a shade over the whole town. Shimla is proud of its past, as displayed on a billboard: "The elegance of yesteryear." As we wandered the streets, people were keen to speak to us. One conversation I had with a very smart Indian gentleman wearing a cravat took me by surprise. He said, "You know what is wrong with India, don't you?" I waited for him to tell me. "The British left."

Here the air was cooler and it was easy to understand why the colonials sought relief from the oppressive heat of Delhi.

For the next five days we travelled deeper into the mountains, en route to Kibber and the start point of our trek. The scenery was stunning, with narrow gorges and wide expansive valleys, hilltop monasteries and little villages. Lush vegetation was replaced with barren rock, sculptured by wind and rain. The days were hot and the nights sticky and uncomfortable.

On several occasions we came across the Indian first minister and his motorcade on a state visit. He took the time to talk to us on our first meeting but after that we had to move to the side of the road to let him pass.

This journey was the first time I had really noticed road signs. As well as conveying a very important message, they are quite amusing:

Drinking whisky makes driving risky!
Don't nag him woman, he's driving.
I am curvaceous, be slow.
It is better to be Mister Late rather than the late mister.

And after some road works,

Sorry for the ooh, ah, ouch, inconvenience.

After arriving in camp each day, we would visit the nearby monastery or village, bathe in the river and wash clothes or play cricket with the crew, well into the evening. The weather, although hot and often uncomfortable, seemed settled.

That is until we started our trek!

Soon after arriving in camp on our first day we were subjected to a thunderstorm with torrential rain. It soon passed. As well as dampening down any dust, it also cleared the atmosphere, allowing for a much more comfortable night.

Unfortunately, it wasn't a lone storm. From then on we were subjected to daily storms with constant thunder and lightning and torrential rain. If we were lucky, we would be in camp before the storm hit, but there were days when we were caught out and suffered the consequences.

On the third day we crossed the Parang La. At 5580m, this was a significant height on only the third day of trekking. But we had been at altitude for at least a week, even if most of it had been spent in vehicles. The descent down the Parang Glacier was fun and took us straight into camp on a grassy patch at the side of the, largely, dry Parang River. The riverbed was extremely wide but the river was confined to a few narrow streams.

The inevitable storm was coming, so before it came I decided to sit on a rock on the riverbed to watch it approach. As the sky darkened with threatening clouds, the lightning forked across the sky, producing loud claps of thunder. It was exhilarating to watch and to listen to the thunder echoing around the mountaintops.

Suddenly, there was a massive crack and a blinding light as a thunderbolt hit the riverbed about one hundred metres in front of me. It was massive, wider than any tree trunk, and, as it hit the ground, stones flew up into the air. It knocked me back off my rock and I could feel the charge in the air. The hairs in my nose seemed to burn and I had a metallic taste in my mouth. Where is the next bolt going to hit? The storm was coming towards me. I decided I had seen enough and took shelter in my tent. The torrential rain hit camp and our grassy patch became sodden. Soon after, the crew quickly dug trenches around the tents to direct the water away from them.

This pattern continued day after day. The mornings were clear, bright and very hot. The cloud built up in the afternoon and exploded into a magnificent storm, plus strong winds, towards the end of the day. River crossings became more difficult as the water began to accumulate in the rivers.

Nothing could distract us from the stunning beauty of the trek and it got even better when we reached the shores of Lake Tsomoriri, a high-altitude lake with crystal-clear waters surrounded by mountains. Those on the far side of the lake formed the border with Tibet.

It took us two and a half days to walk the length of Tsomoriri, into the village of Korzok, the first village we had come across since leaving Kibber. There was a welcome party. The whole village had come out to greet us, the women in national costume, the men in their working clothes and more children than we had bargained for. They had heard that we were going to help them while we were based in their village.

There is no school in Korzok, the nearest school being in a village 40km away. While the Indian government pays for their education, it does not pay for the children to either travel to and from school each day, or for boarding fees. The roads don't allow the children to travel back and forth daily so we had raised some money to pay for the children to board. We handed over 100,000 rupees, which was sufficient for 128 children to board for a year. But it was not an endless supply of money. What would happen the next year? We wanted to encourage other trekkers to contribute, so some of the girls painted a notice indicating how other travellers could help.

In addition, we had lots of goodie bags full of school materials and toys, and a large supply of knitted teddy bears to give to the younger children. As much as we tried to only give one to each child, the mothers played the system. Having received a teddy, they hid it in the folds of their costume while they were given a second. Children were passed around from one adult to another in order to confuse us, and confuse us they did!

Within minutes, two teddies were on display and for sale in the shop next door.

We were not just in Korzok to entertain the local community and support them in their needs. We had another reason for being there. In the range of mountains overlooking Tsomoriri there was a peak, Mentok. At 6250m it was going to prove a significant challenge and also give me another opportunity to climb a peak higher than Angela had achieved. I was acutely aware that the daily thunderstorms would have severely hampered our chances of success, by depositing lots of fresh snow.

Leaving Korzok, we climbed the lower slopes towards base camp. The views of the lake below were breathtaking. The clarity and shade of blue was mesmerising.

By late afternoon, amid sporadic hailstorms, we reached base camp just below the lateral moraine of the Mentok Glacier. It was a cold, desolate place. Climbing up the moraine to have a look at the view and the route, I was not feeling too optimistic about our chances. We had to cross the glacier diagonally in order to reach a snow-filled gully. The angle of the gully was at about 50°, gradually easing as you came out onto the summit dome. We assessed that it would take two hours to cross the glacier, between five and seven hours to climb the gully and another two hours up to the summit. Between nine and eleven hours! A long climb and, with the descent back to camp, making it a very long day.

We spent the rest of the daylight hours fitting crampons and making our plan of campaign, which included a 3.00am wake up call.

As soon as we had eaten, we all drifted off to our tents for an early night.

Sleep was hard to come by. It was very difficult to switch the mind off, thinking about the mammoth task ahead. It started to snow.

When 3.00am came, it was still snowing. Neeraj came to my tent and told me that we would delay until 5.00am.

At 5.00am, nothing had changed, except more snow had fallen and was continuing to fall. We decided to delay until 7.00am.

By the time 7.00am arrived, we could see the extent of the snow. It did not look good. The going would be very slow, and the fact that we had delayed the start by more than four hours meant we would not have enough daylight to get up and back. Also, there was now a huge cornice overhanging the gully. We would be foolish to go up there.

I could see that Neeraj and the crew were unhappy about the situation but they were reluctant to make the call. I took the pressure off them by deciding to abort the attempt. We still had a spare day; should we sit it out and try the next day? The chances were that the conditions would not improve and, if the weather patterns continued to perform as they had in recent days, we would get more snow.

I gathered the group together and gave them the bad news. There was a sombre mood in the mess tent but also an air of resignation. I pointed out that we were out here for twenty-eight days and the summit day was one twenty-eighth of the whole. In that context it was not important. It is more about the journey.

We broke camp and began to head back to Korzok. As we did so, there was a huge CRACK! The cornice overhanging the gully snapped off, sending a destructive avalanche all the way down to the glacier. Phew! Certainly, if we had been in the wrong place at the wrong time, there would have been a very different ending to this story. I would not have wanted to read the headlines in the papers had we proceeded with our plan.

Yet another occasion had passed without me climbing higher than Angela!

The next day we focused on helping out in the community, with some painting and digging rubbish pits and generally tidying up around the camping ground.

The inevitable storm arrived in the late afternoon. We were expecting a couple of buses to arrive during the day, ready to take us back to Leh. But they didn't arrive. The storms had been much worse in other areas of Ladakh and word got through that the buses were stuck in mud.

We, too, were stuck! In Korzok.

Not for long. While we waited, wondering what was going to

happen, Neeraj was busy in the background and managed to procure two tipper lorries, more used to carrying rocks. We piled all our kit into the lorries and then climbed aboard, sitting on the comfortable bags.

Spirits were high as we left, waving farewell to our wonderful hosts, the community of Korzok. It felt as if we were in some sort of disaster movie and were refugees escaping to safety. It was a bumpy ride on unmade roads but we were happy to be on our way.

After some time, we came across a convoy of Land Cruisers that had come out from Leh to meet us. They had had an interesting off-road journey to get to us, avoiding floods and quagmires. We transferred our kit and ourselves to the vehicles and continued in convoy.

After some time we came across two buses stuck in the soft ground, with their drivers asleep across the seats. They were not going to get out without help, so we all piled out and pushed the buses back onto firmer ground. One was much easier than the other and we had to hitch one of the Land Cruisers to give us some help.

Near the lakes at Tsokar the sky turned an inky black and we could see a wall of heavy rain heading towards us. Lightning forked across the darkness. The rain, when it came, was torrential and the Land Cruisers found it difficult to maintain traction. The windscreen wipers struggled to cope with the deluge, so we sought refuge in a lone parachute café in the middle of nowhere. The army in Ladakh have single-use parachutes for dropping supplies. Once the parachutes have been used, they cannot be used again, so many find their way into the hands of local people, who use them as a canopy for a café. They offer not only shelter when it rains but shade from the searing summer sun.

The parachute under which we sheltered was in the middle of a huge basin surrounded by mountains. It was so far off the beaten track. The café owner was a herdsman who had his flock of goats and sheep grazing on the summer pastures. The café gave him an opportunity to make a little extra cash and to meet passing travellers. The rain hammered down on the canvas.

Eventually, the sky brightened and the rain eased sufficiently for us to continue our journey.

Shortly after leaving Tsokar, we rejoined the tarmac road in order to cross the Tanglingtar La. The climb round hairpin bend after hairpin bend went on forever. Many of the bends had streams crossing the road: streams now full of fresh rainfall. Often the water came over the sills of the Land Cruisers and into the footwells.

Eventually, we reached the top of the pass at 5152m. It was in cloud and cold, a sharp contrast to the temperature earlier in the day. There is a sign at the top, which states, "Unbelievable is it not."

The descent down the other side was much quicker, although the road remained high for quite some time. As we descended the streams grew with more and more water, and were becoming incredibly turbulent. Shortly after the village of Gyan, we entered the gorge. Here the river was really violent, and in places merged with the road as the gorge narrowed further.

We soon came to a halt. The road was totally submerged. The raging river now filled right across the floor of the gorge. The water was a grey, silty, swirling mess. The drivers climbed out of their vehicles and walked to the water's edge, where the road disappeared. Time for cigarettes as they assessed the situation. We all climbed out to have a look for ourselves, fearing that we were going to be stuck here until the water levels dropped.

Cigarettes and conversation concluded, the lead driver confirmed that he could get us through. I must have had absolute faith in him because I never once questioned the wisdom of his decision. We all climbed back into our vehicles, anticipating a nerve-wracking experience.

Slowly, we moved forward, carefully following the wake of the vehicle in front. It was taking an age but, after almost 2km, we emerged from the water onto visible tarmac. We had nothing but praise for the drivers. We learnt later that, about half an hour after we passed through the flooded section, the whole lot was lifted, destroyed and the debris carried downstream. We were so lucky.

We eventually emerged into the Indus Valley. The Indus River had burst its banks and the land either side was under water. Many landslides had occurred on the main highway but we managed to get through and reached Leh safely.

Clearly, after this experience, the guidebooks need to be updated; the climate in Ladakh is not as stable as it used to be and travellers need to be aware and prepared for every eventuality. Climate change is taking place.

We saw another example of extreme weather in 2010. Everything had gone so well with the Trans Zanskar Trek. It had often been extremely hot, even at height, and we spent a lot of the time at altitude, crossing nine passes in excess of 5000m.

The night we finished the trek in Lamayuru, we experienced a storm in the middle of the night. It was quite amusing, really. Nearly all of the group had decided to sleep outside under the stars and were caught totally unawares when the heavens opened, forcing them to make a swift dash for their tents.

That storm in itself caused some considerable damage, destroying one or two bridges on the main highway leading to Leh.

In Leh, we had arranged to visit the Druk White Lotus School, adjacent to the Thiksey Monastery. It is a model school, firmly committed to giving young people the tools for success in the modern world while at the same time emphasising the importance of their culture. I had visited the school on previous trips to Ladakh and was extremely impressed with the work they were doing and how the school building was developing with the support of a UK-based architects' firm. The quality of design and the thought put into construction was superb. The classrooms were cool in the summer and warm in the winter. The floors were polished wood, not the usual earth floor that you see in most schools in this region.

On this particular visit we presented the school with lots of educational equipment and materials, toys and money. We spent time with the children, chatting, playing games, teaching and learning songs.

It was our last day in Leh. The following morning we would be flying back to Delhi, not to go home but to enjoy India's Golden Triangle of Delhi, Agra and Jaipur.

At about 1.00am that night there was a storm, an exceptional storm. The rain came down in sheets. I have never witnessed anything like it. Outside our hotel, on a hill, there was a river of water rushing by a foot deep.

After half an hour or so, the torrential rain stopped and I was able to go back to sleep. It was only as we woke up later that we began to realise the full extent of the storm. Mudslides had been triggered on the barren earth above the town and, as they descended on the town, they gathered speed and material. A four-storey hotel collapsed into a heap of rubble. Below that, the bus station was destroyed with buses tipped over and piled up against each other. The mudslide continued to wreak havoc, going on to destroy the telephone exchange, part of the hospital and on to the airport, where the mud finally came to rest across the runway.

We would not be flying out, but we had to head for the airport in order to find out the likely scenario. We queued, along with hundreds of others outside the airport, waiting for news. The doors were locked. Eventually, we were told what we were expecting: there would be no flights today.

Fortunately, we were able to return to our hotels. The group, because there were fifty-two of us, had to spread out between two hotels. Before we separated, I instructed everybody to stay in their hotels, not to venture out into the streets. People were grieving, not only the loss of property; we were aware that at least 200 lives had been lost in the devastation.

I needed to get a message out to the UK. An event like this would surely hit the news at home. I needed to let people know that everybody was safe. How? The internet was down, as were the phones. Foreign mobiles are blocked by the military because of Ladakh's close proximity to sensitive Kashmir. The only way I could do it was to borrow Neeraj's mobile, get one message to Angela and hope she could spread the word.

There was a constant procession of funerals walking past our hotel. From a high point adjacent to the hotel, I looked down where the hotel and bus station used to be, and was grateful that we were all safe.

During the course of the day I learnt that the Druk White Lotus School had been hit by another mudflow and the whole school was covered in two metres of thick mud and rocks. Fortunately, all the children were safe, having been transferred to Thiksey Monastery, on higher ground. The mud flowed in one side of all the classrooms and out of the other, destroying the beautiful woodwork of the construction. All the items we had donated the day before were also destroyed.

That evening a thunderclap and a heavy shower spread panic through the streets of Leh as people fled from their houses, seeking higher ground.

Following our extra night in Leh, we headed to the airport, hoping that we would be able to fly out. The runway had been cleared but flights into Leh were severely restricted. As a result, there were fewer flights out. There was chaos in the airport, with so many people needing to get out. There was a lot of anger and frustration. Forty-three of my group managed to get seats on the first flight. That left nine, including me. I wasn't going to get angry and shout. There is no point. I calmly let the girl behind the check-in desk know of my needs and those of the eight stranded with me, and waited.

There was only one more flight out that day and we got the last nine seats. Luck was on our side, yet again.

I went back to Leh a year later. The death toll from that one storm had risen to nearly 1300 and they were still finding bodies buried in the mud. I also took my group to the Druk White Lotus School, where we rebuilt the destroyed adventure playground and repaired tables and chairs that had been pulled out of the debris.

These mountain areas have always been subject to pretty extreme weather. Ladakh is largely a high-altitude desert, with warm, dry summers and cold, dry winters. It would seem that these are not freak, once-in-a-millennium events; they are happening too often, suggesting a changing weather pattern brought about by a changing climate.

13
—

THE TALE OF THE LOST PASSPORT

Let us start this story in Manali, in the north Indian state of Himachal Pradesh. At just over 2000m it is a Himalayan resort town and the gateway to much higher Himalayan mountains. We had already had issues with lost passports – one left on the coach that took us to Heathrow and only repatriated with its owner because the driver turned round from Warwick Services before check-in closed. Two more had been left in the Connaught Hotel in Delhi but were again repatriated when the hotel couriered them, at no extra cost, to Manali. While annoying, none of these were to test us like the tale I am about to tell.

Manali was just a steppingstone on our journey to trek the Trans Zanskar route from Darcha to Lamayuru, a route that would take us through some really remote Ladakh landscapes and over nine 5000m passes. It was going to be an exciting challenge for the forty-two students and nine staff and medics. It was a big group!

Leaving Manali in a convoy of thirteen Land Cruisers, we worked our way on good roads, through alpine scenery towards the Rotang Pass, one of the highest stretches of road in the world. There was an air of excitement and anticipation for the journey ahead of us, following the Zanskar River. Unfortunately, as we approached the foot of the pass, we could not help but notice that there was a stationary line of traffic winding its way up the many hairpins on the rapidly deteriorating road surface. Soon we found ourselves, only a short distance into our climb over the Rotang, at the back of that queue. It was apparent that we were not going anywhere very fast.

Instead of sitting there, many of us climbed out of our vehicles to stretch our legs. Gradually news of the cause of the delay filtered down the line of traffic. An oil tanker had collided with another vehicle and was precariously hanging from the road, ready to cartwheel down the slope at the slightest provocation. The army was in situ, trying to haul the lorry back up the slope and onto the road. Should the lorry decide to allow gravity to take its course, it would inevitably come into contact with vehicles below.

Anticipating that we would be there for some time, we all found ways to while away the time – reading, catching up on our diaries, wandering up and down the side of the road meeting individuals and family groups caught up in the delay. Many of the boys in the group embarked upon a game on their phones, creating quite tense competition in each of the vehicles.

After a few hours, Rishi, one of our guides, decided to collect everybody's passports so he could note down the pertinent details in preparation for the checkpoint when we eventually reached the top of the pass. Having taken the information, he returned the passports to their rightful owners.

We spent six hours stationary in the queue, six hours that would probably prevent us from reaching Darcha. Although they had not managed to bring the lorry up onto the road, they had created enough room for smaller vehicles to pass, thus easing the congestion and leaving only lorries and buses still stuck on the hill.

Slowly, we edged our way up, eventually passing the stricken vehicle. We later learnt that, having cleared the road of vehicles, the army decided the tanker was irretrievable and let it go, allowing it to tumble down the hill to a final resting place.

By the time we reached the top of the Rotang Pass it was dark. There was a need to stop for a while for passport control, but, as Rishi had done all the paperwork earlier, it did not take long, just long enough for us to stretch our legs before enduring the long, winding descent. It was obvious we were not going to make it to Darcha. Soon after reaching the foot of the pass, we pulled off the road onto a relatively flat area of grass, where we pitched tents and the cooks prepared a meal.

It was while we were pitching the tents that I was approached by one of the boys, saying that he could not find his passport. I asked him the obvious question, "What did you do with it when Rishi returned it?"

"Put it into my kitbag."

"Are you sure?" I asked.

"Yes," came the confident reply.

"In that case it will turn up. It's a bit dark to go searching for it now; we'll find it in the morning."

The following morning the boy went through his kitbag and there was no sign of the passport. Putting a large blue tarpaulin on the ground, we did the same with those who had shared the vehicle with him. At the same time, others checked all the vehicles and the area around each vehicle. The passport was nowhere to be found!

This presented us with a problem, a problem that had to be carefully managed.

The first challenge was getting through the checkpoint at Darcha. To be honest, it wasn't a very stringent checkpoint. They were not going to notice that one passport was missing and, after a perfunctory glance at both the paperwork and us, they waved us through. Having bypassed this first hurdle, we decided to phone the British Consulate in Delhi to find out what we needed to do to obtain a new passport. We would have to visit the consulate in person for an interview and for the passport to be issued. It would take ten days to complete the formalities. We would then have to apply for an exit visa, which would take a further four days.

As luck would have it, halfway through our trek, we would come across the town of Padam. There, the passportless boy and I could take the bus to Leh, where we could get a flight to Delhi. While the rest of the group completed the trek, we would kick our heels in Delhi, awaiting the passport, by which time the group would have also arrived in Delhi. While waiting for the exit visa, we could rejoin the group for the short trip around the Golden Triangle. It worked. The timing fitted in with the schedule for the trip. What could go wrong?

After ten days of trekking we reached Padam. As this was the largest settlement on our journey, we had decided to have a couple of rest days. This would give us time to organise the bus to Leh and put our plan into effect. While the group and crew played cricket, I thought it prudent that we report the loss of the passport to the police, there being a police post in town.

Finding the police post, we ventured inside. There, we met the local constabulary, a smartly dressed officer, rather out of place with the rest of Padam. He was clearly very proud of his position.

Reporting the loss, he asked, "A British passport?"

"Yes," I replied.

"It's been found," he said with a degree of pride.

Feeling very excited, I asked, "Where?"

"It was found in the mud on the top of the Rotang Pass. You are very lucky it was found as it was almost buried."

"That is wonderful news! Where is the passport now?" I asked, hoping he would produce it from his desk drawer.

"It's in Leh. I told the person who found it to take it to the tourist information office in Leh."

Hiding my disappointment, I said, "That's great. Thank you so much." I would have preferred to have been given it there and then, but having it in Leh was the next best thing.

If the passport was in Leh, we could all finish the trek. There was no need now for us to go to Delhi, to kick our heels wasting time, let alone the waste of money such a trip would have incurred.

Later that day the policeman came to camp to watch the cricket match. While standing on the makeshift boundary, I could not help but notice him eyeing up and fondling a set of walking poles. Later, just as he was about to leave, I presented him with the walking poles to show our appreciation for his help.

The next ten days saw us crossing high pass after high pass, and between each pass dropping down to the roaring waters of the Zanskar River. The scenery was truly spectacular. To think, there are plans to build a road through the Zanskar Valley that would ruin the peace and tranquillity of this truly remote region forever.

The trek finally came to an end, giving us all a great sense of achievement. It had been extremely hard at times and, with Padam being the only feasible escape, everybody had displayed a great level of commitment. There was good reason to want to celebrate, but, before I could relax, I needed to get my hands on a passport.

On the first full day in Leh I visited the tourist information office. There, behind a large desk, sat a bespectacled gentleman in a shirt and tie. The room oozed with his own self-importance.

Introducing myself, I asked if he could give me the British passport that had been handed to him.

"I don't have it."

"You don't have it? Who does have it?" I asked with a feeling of foreboding creeping into my voice.

"The honest and kind Indian gentleman who found it. I told him to look after it."

"Do you have his name, his contact details?" I asked, already fearing that I knew the answer.

"No!"

There was nothing more to say. Now, with only five days left in India, we had at least a fourteen-day process to manage. I had a trip to Turkey with a group as soon as I returned from India. Other staff had family plans already arranged. Could the boy's mother come out to look after him while he waited for his passport? No; she would not be able to get a visa in time. The only solution, and it was not ideal, was for our tour providers to host him. I trusted them implicitly, but is trust alone enough?

While pondering all the options available, as well as those that were not, we suddenly came upon the idea of the local radio station. In fact, the first question was, "Is there a local radio station?" Yes, there was. What if we were to put out an appeal on the radio for the finder of the passport to return it to the tourist information office? It was certainly worth a try.

Putting out an appeal, we waited.

The following morning we received a message from the tourist information office that they had the passport. I said we would be along to collect it immediately.

"I don't think he should have it," came the stern reply from the officer we had spoken to previously.

"How much is it going to cost us?" I asked, feeling annoyed by petty Indian bureaucracy.

"Oh, I don't want money," retorted the officer with an air of superiority. How could we possibly think of him as being corrupt? "I want a letter from the boy saying how sorry he is, how stupid he has been and how grateful he is to the honest Indian nation for returning his passport."

I decided, to speed things along, to write the grovelling letter for him, partly because he could not be found.

Having written it, I found the boy in question, got him to sign the letter, and took him with me to the tourist information office. The superior bespectacled gentleman took the letter proffered to him by the boy and read it carefully while we waited in silence, our hearts racing in anticipation.

Eventually he looked up beyond the piece of paper, pointed a bony finger at the boy and said, "I want him to write it!"

Flushed with embarrassment, the letter was rewritten at a vacant desk, while I, and the officer, waited in awkward silence.

Once the letter was written it was handed over and we, in turn, were, somewhat reluctantly given a rather shoddy, mud-stained

British passport. It summed up how I felt. This lost passport had taken up a huge amount of my time, energy and thoughts. With the passport back I could now enjoy the remainder of the trip, the return to Delhi for the Golden Triangle.

That night a massive storm hit Leh and the surrounding area, triggering mudslides that destroyed and engulfed many buildings, sadly causing the loss of many lives. One mudslide crossed the runway at the airport, preventing any planes from landing or taking off. You already know about that.

14

SHARE THE VISION

One morning, in 2005 or 2006, I was watching the news on the BBC. During the broadcast there was an item that caught my attention. A young blind boy from Britain was reporting from somewhere in Africa. He had won a competition and the reward was a trip to Africa and an opportunity to make a filmed report for the BBC.

This started me thinking, "What is there to stop young blind people from doing everything that their sighted counterparts can do, if the proper measures are put in place?" The idea really excited me, partly because I have had very little to do with disability throughout my life. If I am honest, it is something I was likely to avoid getting involved with, because I have been uncomfortable dealing with it. I have always been full of admiration for anybody who devotes their energy and time to working or helping the disabled.

I convinced myself that, if we had a group of blind or visually impaired students and paired them with sighted students, we could make it work.

I did not have to look far to test my idea. I contacted New College Worcester, an independent secondary boarding and day school for blind and visually impaired children. I spoke to their head of outdoor education, Caroline. Would she like to come round to see me and I could show her pictures of destinations I had in mind? Caroline, quite rightly, was reluctant to commit to visiting me at home: "How do I know you are not the mad axeman of Worcester?" I went to visit her at the college, leaving my axe at home!

I needed her to be involved. I could not do this without her expertise. Fortunately, Caroline was as keen as me to see this succeed and we took tentative steps towards getting a group together. We envisaged a small, manageable group so we chose six students from New College Worcester who would be paired with six students from King's School Worcester.

This needed careful planning and preparation. The sighted had to understand the needs of the blind and visually impaired students, to learn guiding techniques and the importance of language. It would be no good if we took these students to a mountainous, culturally different destination if they had no concept of where they were. The visually impaired developed complete trust and faith in those guiding them, to know that they were always safe. Equally, the sighted students became aware of the many similarities between them.

Of course, questions were on the minds of the guides: "Just how much help do they need? Do we have to help them with everything?"

We were soon to learn that blind and visually impaired young people are fiercely independent. They will endeavour to do everything for themselves. It is only when they are in a strange environment, a place never visited before, that they need help.

We also learnt that they are the same as all teenagers, liking the same pop music as the rest of us, are attached to social media, have the same likes and dislikes, and look for ways to break the rules.

Of course, while we have all of our senses and use them all equally, the lack of sight enhances their other senses to provide some compensation for not being able to see.

As part of our training, we introduced the group to an obstacle course, with the guides leading. Most often, words are enough to bypass an obstacle. It is only when there is a fear of falling that there needs to be extra care taken. Then we reversed roles and the blind led their guides, who, at this time, were blindfolded. Now the other senses came into play: varying levels of shade suggested a tree or a wall, sound bouncing back from a surface in the way, and changes of temperature, none of which were discernible to us but were obvious to the visually impaired.

We had to get to know each other socially as well, so we arranged to go out for meals, to go ten-pin bowling and tandem bike riding. The emphasis was always to have fun together, to develop strong, trusting relationships among people who were happy in each other's company.

The real test came when we took the group camping, mainly in Wales. We took them out onto the hills in all weather, tested their skills and gave the students opportunities they might not otherwise have had.

People would see us out on the hills, Pen-y-fan or Snowdon. They may not, at first, have realised that some of the group were blind, but, once they did, they would be full of admiration for what the young people were doing.

There was one occasion when we experienced the reverse. Blind people do not move as quickly as sighted people and cannot be aware of everything around them, even with a guide. We were descending Snowdon towards Llanberis. It was busy, mainly because there was a triathlon event taking place. As one of the competitors came running behind us, he shouted, "Get out of the fucking way!" I was incensed. How dare he? I was all for chasing him down the mountain, if I could have caught up with him. Thinking about it, if he had known he was shouting at blind people, he might well have been mortified at doing so. I hope so.

Following the training with the initial group, we started a two-year cycle, first visiting Morocco in 2007, trekking through the wonderful rock formations of the Jebel Sahro, a range of mountains that lie between the High Atlas Mountains and the Sahara Desert. Although hard at times, particularly on the first day, it was a perfect introduction to the concept of "Share the Vision" and proved that blind and visually impaired young people can go on expedition.

From the end of the trek we travelled deeper into the Sahara to trek into a beautiful area of golden sand dunes. The experience of struggling up the shifting sands and rolling down was a great tactile experience, even if a number of cameras succumbed to sand in the works! We used camels on this part of the trek to carry our kit and also the group were able to experience riding these ships of the desert.

They may not have been able to see the night sky clearly, but the experience of sleeping under the stars was unforgettable. One visually impaired boy was overjoyed. He had never seen stars before because in the urban environments of home there is always too much light pollution. In the desert, the stars were so vivid, he could see them for the first time.

Scrambling over mountains and rolling down sand dunes was easy compared to coping with crossing the road in Marrakesh. Traffic in Morocco is not as disciplined as it is at home, and zebra crossings mean nothing to a driver, who will happily skirt round pedestrians. We found this far more stressful than the great outdoors.

We followed Morocco with an ambitious trip to Nepal. The first challenge was taking a long-haul flight.

Our trek was in the Annapurna foothills, going as high as Poon Hill, where we were to be for sunrise. Not all the blind students climbed Poon Hill; starting in the dark was too difficult to manage and we would never have got there in time. It was, largely, a reward for the guides.

Sunrise from Poon Hill is spectacular. The first shades of light appear from behind Machhapuchare (Fish Tail) mountain. As the glow increases, the light begins to catch the summits of the Annapurnas, directly in front of us and across to Dhaulagiri to the west. The sun cannot come soon enough; it is really cold until the first rays begin to warm us. By then the mountains are in their full glory, while below the red flowers of the rhododendron shine like beacons from the slopes.

We were always on the lookout for tactile experiences. In Kathmandu it was the many statues to deities that could be touched. The shapes and smoothness of the metal or stone gave them an impression of the culture they were immersing themselves in. Traffic was, again, the most dangerous aspect, particularly in a place like Kathmandu, where there is an expectation for pedestrians to share the space with bicycles, rickshaws, motorbikes and cars!

The Chitwan National Park also provided tactile experiences, journeys sitting in the back of an ox cart or, best of all, riding elephants, touching their trunks and bathing them in the river.

We were now flushed with the success of these trips. Not just the trips but with the concept of providing young people with disability the opportunity to explore the world. I wanted to expand the idea. I wrote to every blind institution in the country, sent copies of films I had made, hoping that they felt it would be something that they could replicate with a local school in their area. Not one replied. I began to ask myself: why? I can only assume that it wasn't a risk they were prepared to take. Perhaps they did not have the staff who felt they could confidently manage such an idea. I began to realise how lucky I was to have found Caroline and Phil and the fact that they worked in a forward-thinking and ambitious school for the blind.

We returned to Morocco in 2011 for a trek in the Anti Atlas that saw us climb a challenging, boulder-strewn 3000m summit.

The second part of the trip took us to the Atlantic coast, where we embarked on a camel trek through the Argon Forest, along sandy beaches with the sound of Atlantic breakers. Camping on the beach was very special.

We ended up in Essaouira, a historical coastal resort. Walking round the souk, we found all the shopkeepers very helpful, allowing the students to touch, to smell and to appreciate what they were buying.

It was while walking back to the hotel, along the esplanade, with three blind students, that we came across a street hawker. I first became aware of him when I felt something on my shoulder.

Looking round, I came face to face with a chameleon. I immediately pointed out that my companions were blind. Could they feel the chameleon? He was extremely obliging and gave his time to each one in turn.

On the sea wall, he had a tray of cakes. I thought it would be appropriate to buy some from him for the time he had devoted to the students. As I did so, he warned me away from some chocolate cakes because they had cannabis in them. I continued to choose!

Suddenly, close behind me a voice rang out. "I wouldn't buy any of those. They have cannabis in them. I wouldn't give them to my children."

"Oh, really?" I said, rather taken aback.

He was gone before I could say, "Not to worry, they're not my children. It's a school trip!"

We ate the cakes that night and nobody started to hallucinate, or feel different in any way.

Our last two trips took us to Iceland. There we undertook to complete the Laugavegur Trek from Landmannalaugar to Thorsmork, a 55km trek taken over four days. This provided a whole range of experiences while travelling through this amazing landscape. Bubbling pools of sulphurous mud, steam vents, fording ice-cold rivers and much, much more. In 2013, we attempted to extend the trek by crossing the crater of Eyjafjallajökull, the volcano that grounded half the world's airlines. Very bad weather and difficult terrain forced us to retreat. I crossed it in 2014 and it would have been too difficult, so I am glad we were forced back.

For such a small country, Iceland has so many features that lend itself to a trip with the visually impaired. Yes, the trekking can be difficult, but no more so than in Nepal or Morocco. It has geysers, hot springs that they can immerse themselves in, even when the air temperature is low, mud pools, glaciers and the most amazing waterfalls. They are huge, with vast amounts of water thunderously cascading down. To feel the blast of cold air and the fine spray amid the noise is just sensational. Skogarfoss has a 62m vertical drop,

Gullfoss tumbles into a gorge and you can walk behind Seljalandsfoss. They all provide perfect sensory experiences.

Perhaps the best way to experience the rivers of Iceland is to white-water raft on them. Not being able to see makes it more heart-in-the-mouth than if you can see. When to paddle, when to hang on and how to read the water in order to prevent falling out are all things that, as a sighted person, you take for granted.

The real test of courage is climbing out of the raft into a gorge along the river, clambering up to the top of the cliff and then, holding hands with your guide, jumping 7m into the river below. The temperature of the water is about 4°C, and, even with a wetsuit on, it is still a shock to the system. A real leap of faith!

Sadly, these trips no longer occur. Changes in personnel at both schools means that they no longer have the staff who are prepared to go. This saddens me, as we have proved, over the five trips, that blind and visually impaired young people can do far more. It has been an excellent and exhilarating series of projects, thoroughly enjoyed by all who participated. They deserve the opportunity.

15

—

OOPS!

When I retired from teaching I decided to replicate some of the training experiences I had provided to students, for adult groups as well, adding a few improvements to make it more comfortable. I had all the equipment, tents etc., and what I didn't have I was happy to buy. It was a lot of fun buying large shelters, big gas burners, tables, chairs, crockery and all the cooking pots and utensils you could possibly need.

I wanted to create a journey, a linear trek that started at A and finished at B. For each trek I would determine where the camps should be, so that a base was created for us to travel from and back to each day. This required transport to manage the logistics. For each trip, I would hire a van to carry all the kit and a minibus to transport the "clients".

To help I had my wife, Angela, and my friend and trekking companion David Thomas. We needed a snappy name, Adventure Guide being a bit lengthy. We came up with T.W.A.T.S. (Thomas, Walton, Angela Trekking Services). David's wife, Annie, joined in later, so we became T.W.A.A.T.S.

Over the years we achieved some creditable long-distance

treks including Hadrian's Wall, St Cuthbert's Way, the Dales Way, Pembrokeshire Coast Path, the Wessex Ridgeway, the Cotswold Diamond Way, Offa's Dyke, the Two Moors Way and the Jurassic Coast Path. These proved enormous fun and people came year after year.

To ensure smooth running, David and I would set up camp ready for Angela arriving with the group. Angela would then be responsible for catering and purchasing, while David and I would concentrate on managing the walks.

Angela is an excellent driver. At no time when she is driving have I felt unsafe. Often, when I am driving, her hands go out to grab the dashboard in preparation for hitting the car in front. Basically, she doesn't trust me, while I have complete trust in her. Or I did!

I don't have an explanation for her behaviour, but when Angela gets behind the wheel of a seventeen-seater minibus she thinks she is in a sports car, driving too fast when approaching a bend and swinging the vehicle round without a care for those sitting behind her. One or two of our "clients" have slightly tender stomachs when it comes to road travel.

It all went wrong in 2015 when we had finished the Dales Way. The lanes are quite narrow in the Yorkshire Dales and even I was feeling queasy on occasion. We had been camping in Dent and had just struck camp when I quietly announced, "I'm not letting Angela drive the minibus today. She throws it round corners far too fast."

Unfortunately, I didn't say it quietly enough and I didn't realise that Angela was not too far behind me.

"I'm going with David!" she said frostily, and stomped off in the direction of David's car.

"Do you think she heard me?" I asked meekly.

Those around me all nodded, suppressing a smile.

It was a wet morning. We all prepared to leave, Angela with David, and the rest of the group in the minibus with me.

David was off like a shot. I had to manoeuvre the minibus, and, in doing so, backed into a drystone wall! "Oh shit!"

I jumped out to see what the damage was. As I did, so I saw thirteen people quickly texting Angela with the news. The damage was minimal but it still cost me a few hundred pounds! And a lot of chagrin.

On St Cuthbert's Way in 2016 we based ourselves at a campsite on the outskirts of Wooler. On the campsite website it says very clearly that groups are not allowed. It was ideally situated and there was very little in the way of an alternative. When I was planning the walk, I purposely visited the site to explain what the group would be doing and how helpful it would be if they would allow us to camp there. I could not have found them more helpful, and they welcomed us with open arms.

All had gone well, although the weather had not been brilliant. A little wire-haired Jack Russell, Dodja, which had come with one of the group, had disgraced himself by chasing the free-range ducks around the camp. I don't think he caught any but there were tell-tale clusters of feathers where there had been a scuffle.

When we returned to camp, having had a soggy last day walking to Lindisfarne, there was a group of motorcyclists camped next to us. There is always something slightly intimidating about motorcyclists, particularly when they wear all their leathers. I know a few and they are the nicest people you could ever meet.

The following morning, we were striking camp and packing everything away. The minibus was in the way so I jumped into the driver's seat to move it. All that was needed was to reverse it in an arc so that it would be facing the right way when it was time to leave.

I had completed the manoeuvre and was just climbing out of the vehicle, when an irate woman confronted me: "What have you done that for?'

"Done what?" I asked. I had been aware of a tent in my rear-view mirror, conscious that I didn't want to run over a sleeping biker.

"Knock his bloody bike over!" she shouted.

"What bike? I haven't seen a bike."

I walked round to the back of the bus, aware that other bikers were beginning to take notice and gather round. There, behind the bus, lying on its side with one handlebar in the mud, was a classic motorcycle.

"I'm sorry, I really didn't see it. I was making sure I didn't hit the tent; I didn't see the bike."

"You drove like a maniac! Do you know what that bike is worth?"

Oh, how I wanted the earth to open up and swallow me. Hearing the commotion, the owner emerged from his tent, horrified to see his bike on its side. A number of expletives were directed towards me while he checked for damage. In fact, all the bikers checked it for damage, scrutinising it in fine detail for something they could nail me for.

"I must have only nudged it. I didn't hear it and there is no mark on the bus. All I can do is apologise. I'm sorry." I repeated.

One by one, they confirmed that there was no damage to the bike and a wave of relief passed over me.

Eventually, everything calmed down and they went about their breakfast while I willed everybody to pack everything away as quickly as possible. I didn't want to experience any more embarrassment.

To appease the group of motorbike enthusiasts, we gave them leftover food from our camp. We left on good terms but I couldn't wait to get away. As I drove away I could relax. My mind drifted to my friend Rob and his Harley-Davidson. He had recently been to a Harley convention in Austria, where there were thousands of bikes lined up. A smile crossed my face. Just imagine the mayhem I could cause by nudging one and setting off the domino effect!

Just for the record, Angela also had a couple of incidents in minibuses, but we don't talk about those.

I haven't confined my "oops" moments solely to minibuses. They have occurred on water, too.

For a number of years I have been organising canoe trips down the River Wye, ranging from one day, as a taster, to four-day, 90-mile trips. The Wye is a very beautiful river, passing through some stunning countryside. To see kingfisher on the riverbanks, salmon leaping and, on one occasion, an otter swim across my bows is just magical.

I have also enjoyed watching friends have fun and provide comical moments. To see two heads bobbing down the rapids at Symonds Yat, having spilled from their canoe, was fun.

There was one occasion that involved Rob of the Harley-Davidson. Everything was going really well when we reached Ross-on-Wye, having paddled for three and a half hours. Pulling up at the landing platform, by the Hope and Anchor, we prepared to go ashore for lunch. There were a number of mothers and children on the jetty, feeding ducks. Suddenly, a horror show opened up in front of them. Rob managed to get one foot in the water and was preparing to swing his other out of the canoe when his foot in the water slipped. Grabbing the nearest thing to him in the hope that he could save himself, he grabbed the canoe, unbalancing Steve to the point where he thought he was going to fall in. The canoe drifted away under Rob's weight, splitting his legs further apart, to the point where his rear became his centre of gravity, whereupon nothing could save him. There was muted laughter from the mothers, not sure if they should express their mirth, until they heard Steve, Ian and me falling about with laughter. I was laughing so much I forgot to get the camera out to record Rob's embarrassment for posterity. The mothers melted away to give counselling to their traumatised children!

I had managed to accomplish a number of canoe trips down the Wye without personal embarrassment. I was pleased with my record. That is, until 2019.

I had led a four-day trip and experienced a friend and his stepdaughter coming to grief by Kerne Bridge. Water levels were low following a fairly dry summer and, just on the downstream side of the bridge, the river narrowed into a fast-flowing channel on a sweeping bend. Sticking out from the bank just above water level there was a sawn-off tree trunk, which proved hazardous for my friends, tipping them out.

The following week, leading another group, I gathered everybody by Kerne Bridge and talked them through this next section, advising them to leave enough distance between each canoe and watch out for the tree, although, from where I was speaking, I couldn't see it.

While I was talking, another group came along with an instructor. I set my group off, Angela and our friend Chris going last. I was not happy with the line they were taking, fearing a capsize was about to happen. I turned to the other instructor and said, "It's always embarrassing when your wife doesn't listen to instruction." With that they negotiated the sweeping bend with ease.

I set off. As soon as I did so, I realised that I had drifted slightly too far downstream and I was approaching at the wrong angle. I hit the tree, now just below the surface, and it tipped me out immediately. It was much deeper than I had anticipated. My foot groped for the stones on the riverbed. Standing on tiptoe, my head was just above the water, an impossible position to try to recover myself and the canoe. The canoe was wedged under the offending piece of tree and I could not muster the leverage to release it.

The instructor of the other group came to my rescue, released my canoe, put it across his own, upside down, to empty out the water, returned it to the water the right way up and handed it to me to walk into the shallows. How embarrassed did I feel? I thanked him for his help, but I really wanted him and his group to go away. My embarrassment was complete.

The next day I shared my canoe with Angela. All had been going really well until we got to Monmouth Bridge. Here the river is quite wide but much of its width is too shallow to navigate, even in a canoe. Angela and I were in the lead canoe and we headed for a narrow channel of fast-flowing water tucked in against the left bank. We aimed for it but got too close into the bank and an overhanging willow tree. I shouted out, "Paddle left! Paddle left!" meaning paddle on the left side. Unfortunately, to Angela, that meant paddle on the right to turn left. It was not my intention that we should explore the tree closely but the flow made it impossible for us to avoid it. In the middle of the foliage was a thick, cut-off trunk, which stopped us dead in the water and tipped Angela over the side, quickly followed by me, with the canoe ending up upside down. It was so funny to see Angela with a bemused look on her face, her sunglasses askew, having been fully submerged. Our so-called friends in the canoes behind, as well as coming to our rescue, were highly amused by our spectacular exit from our canoe.

Angela has since received enormous amounts of sympathy, while I have had nothing but stick! Well, if it makes them happy.

16

—

TIBET

When I think of Tibet I have very mixed emotions. Tibet has provided me with some really positive memories but, at the same time, some of my worst memories come from this fascinating part of the world. I feel anger when I see and hear what the Chinese are doing surreptitiously to undermine Tibetan culture, to take away their identity, much the same as they are doing to the Uyghurs in the west.

On the surface, you see new housing, whole villages having been flattened to allow for the construction of corporate, uniform housing. These do, perhaps, provide a better standard of living for the Tibetans, but it is an improvement that is being imposed upon them.

There were three years separating my visits to Tibet and the changes I saw were phenomenal. Firstly, the high-speed railway has reached Lhasa. In 2004 it was nothing more than concrete columns rising up out of the frozen earth. In 2007 it was completed, two years ahead of schedule, bringing in hundreds of Chinese workers relocating to Tibet.

The road system is expanding beyond belief. In 2004 I travelled by road from Lhasa to Everest Base Camp, a distance of about 380km;

290km of that journey was on unmade roads. In 2007, all but about 80km had been turned into smooth, well-constructed highways.

Some of my best interactions with people have been in Tibet. I was buying some items from a stallholder in Lhasa who wanted to know if I was married. When I told her I was, she asked if I was pregnant! I wasn't sure it showed that much.

As we approached one of the gateways to Drepung Monastery, just outside Lhasa, there was a young girl and her brother with an elderly couple. The girl asked, "May I speak English with you?" Angela spoke for the rest of us, agreeing to chat. A charming conversation took place, with many questions going back and forth. She was eleven and her brother thirteen, but it was she who had the confidence and the ability to converse with us.

They followed us as we continued on our tour, and, as it was drawing to an end, she engaged us in conversation again. Her grandfather, who stood very much in the background, had taught her English. Her grandmother, who spoke little, was the one who kept encouraging her granddaughter to perpetuate the conversation. She started to tell us the history of Drepung Monastery, and then moved on to the Jokhang Monastery, the Potala Palace and, finally Sera Monastery. When she had told us all she could, she asked, "Can I sing a song to you?" Could we stop her, now that she had reached full momentum?

She started to sing "If You're Happy and You Know It Clap Your Hands". The Himalayan Club theme song! Her brother quickly joined in. They followed it with "Mary's Boy Child" and concluded with "Home on the Range". What a mix!

When we offered her money, she refused, saying, "I don't speak for money. I do it to practise my English."

We can, and do, go round many monasteries in our travels and it is impossible to get to grips with the basics of any religion, let alone Buddhism. We will forget the various statues of Buddha that we saw at Drepung Monastery but our encounter with the girl who longed to speak English will remain with us for ever.

When we went to Shishipangma Base Camp in 2004 we came across a group of children who had come to see us in camp. They were quite shy at first and it took a little encouragement for them to feel comfortable with us. A number of them had plasters on their temples and foreheads. I was intrigued to know why. Adults had asked us for plasters on other occasions. They wear them for headaches. They don't have pills for headaches but believe that, if they put a plaster on the area of most pain, the headache will be cured. The children were as intrigued with us as we with them. Conversation was difficult but they enjoyed touching things that belonged to us.

That also proved the case in a school we visited in Kharta. We were there with "goodie bags" containing the usual school, toy and hygiene items. Having distributed them, we were invited into a classroom with, at least, sixty children packed in on benches. Having given out the gifts, the children separated us from anything hanging from our rucksacks! It took us a while to realise that our mascots had disappeared and there was no way we were going to get them back. Unlike the children we met near Shishipangma, these children were rogues and had learnt how to make the most of any opportunity that came along.

I have seen some poverty in my travels, but none like that seen in Tibet. A group of us sat at a table in a roadside restaurant with a meal. The restaurant was a scruffy hole and the food was barely edible. Throughout our meal a young mother with a baby sat at our feet, begging for us to throw her scraps of food. It was a pathetic sight. She was behaving just like the feral dogs in this part of the world. None of us could bring ourselves to give her food. We did, however, find out what a mother and baby most want. Butter. Tibetan butter is revolting and is one of the main ingredients in Tibetan tea. It is undrinkable. Tibetans love it. It takes away the pains of hunger. It is also used as a lotion, smeared on the cheeks and forehead, providing protection from the fierce sun and biting winds that occur on the Tibetan plateau. We bought her a large slab of butter, which pleased her, but I will never forget the pathetic figure she portrayed at our feet.

We chose to fly to Lhasa from Kathmandu. On both occasions the sky has been cloudless, providing us with incredible views of the Himalayas, as we first flew east along its length, before crossing close to Everest. Then, having crossed the high peaks, we flew over the high-altitude desert of the Tibetan plateau, with occasional snow-capped peaks jutting out of it. Astounding!

Arrival at Lhasa Airport is interesting, and a little intimidating. For ease, we have a group visa, but we have to line up exactly as the names appear on the visa, in alphabetical order. Woe betide anybody trying to get through out of order. Their command of English is not that good. I was asked, "Where your declaration?"

"What declaration?" I thought. Do I have to give a declaration of loyalty to the Communist Party? To China? Somebody help me here.

It transpired that they wanted to know if I had anything to declare. Phew!

Lhasa is nothing like I expected. The old city was as expected, if not better, but there is also a modern city with glass-fronted office blocks, wide roads and fast-moving traffic. We were staying in the old part of town in the Dhood Gu Hotel, a colourfully painted and traditionally carved Tibetan hotel, without a lift. I refer to the lack of a lift because Lhasa is 3700m above sea level and it is tiring going up to the fourth floor.

During the Chinese invasion in 1959 and the years that followed, many of the monasteries were damaged. Monks were tortured, icons destroyed and a lot of the paintings of people and animals that adorn the walls of monasteries had their eyes gouged out. There is still evidence of this today, although the Chinese have allowed some monasteries to be restored.

It was while at Drepung Monastery, once home to 10,000 monks, that I asked our guide about the Chinese in Tibet. He quickly cut me short. "I cannot answer your questions. You never know who is listening."

Also, while at Drepung, we were able to watch the monks gather for prayers. Horns blare and cymbals clash. While the most senior monks perform the ceremony, the other monks listen and respond appropriately. It was interesting to see that one boy monk was surreptitiously playing with his Game Boy in the folds of his habit.

The monasteries are the highlight of Lhasa, the most prominent being Potala Palace, perched high on a hill overlooking the city. It is truly magnificent, a pinch-me moment. I am actually here, standing in front of the Potala Palace.

There are one thousand rooms in the palace but the public can only visit about a dozen. There are Chinese guards wherever you go, ensuring that you do not take any pictures and you behave appropriately. Unfortunately, as you do the kora around the perimeter of the palace, there are lots of stalls, run by Chinese, selling cheap, nasty goods.

While it is magnificent to look up at and to look down from, it lacks warmth. It is not my favourite. There are four that I would say are more interesting. I have already mentioned Drepung. Of the others, Jokhang, in the centre of the old city, is the most holy site for Tibetans. Many Tibetans constantly do a kora around the perimeter, the most devout prostrating themselves as they pray and circumnavigating the monastery. Others pray at the front of the monastery, again prostrating many times. They wear protective pads on their hands.

I don't think I have ever come across such a devout group of people who demonstrate absolute faith. It is very humbling and emotional to watch them, knowing that many of them have pretty wretched lives, and that the Chinese are watching them all the time. Guards are never very far away and the peace is occasionally shattered by barked Chinese orders from tannoy speakers mounted on a post close to the worshippers.

In the hills, outside Lhasa, there are two small monasteries that I find much more interesting. The first is Sera Monastery, where, each afternoon, about two hundred monks gather in the courtyard and hold debates. They sit in groups of four or five. One from each group stands and starts a debate. He emphasises his point by stamping his foot and slapping his hands, then sliding his upper hand to the armpit of the lower arm. It creates a cacophony of voices and slaps, which get louder and louder as the arguments develop. There is no way of knowing what they are debating, but it could have been politics, religion, philosophy, astronomy or, possibly, judging from the glances we received, us. Despite some discussions becoming heated, it was all good-natured. It is a wonderful piece of theatre.

Suddenly, a bell rings and the debates come to an abrupt end. The monks rise and arrange themselves in a circle around a senior monk. Once they are all seated on the ground, the monk then speaks to them at some length. All eyes are on the speaker, apart from a few monks near the back of the circle, who persist in throwing pebbles at each other!

In 2013 I was walking through the narrow streets of Thamel, in Kathmandu, when a young man walking towards me developed a broad grin across his face. It was a grin of recognition, although I had no idea who he was. He stopped me in my tracks, shaking my hand. Anticipating this was a set routine in order to obtain money from tourists, I was on my guard.

"I'm sorry, I don't know you. Have we met?" I tentatively asked.

Still with his broad grin, he replied, "No, we have not met, but I remember you. You came to Sera Monastery in 2007 and took many photos. I was a monk there."

"Wow! You have an excellent memory."

"I never forget a face."

We exchanged a few more pleasantries, before parting and going our separate ways.

The other monastery is even smaller but carries out a fascinating public service, sky burials.

It had been badly damaged during the Cultural Revolution, paintings particularly. A group of monks were lovingly restoring the artworks, which were in various stages of development. The walls, having been replastered, have pencil drawings as a guide for the painters. The detail is phenomenal and it was fascinating watching the painstaking work performed by these monks.

Outside, on the open hillside, there is a large, white-painted rock. When a corpse is brought to the monastery for a sky burial, it is taken up to the rock, whereupon the monks hack it into small pieces. Nothing was happening while we were there but there were about three hundred vultures sitting in a line along the ridgetop overlooking the valley. They clearly know where to hang out.

When a body is offered for sky burial, it does not take long for that number of vultures to dispose of it. It becomes a massive feeding frenzy. By the time the deed is done, the vultures are so full, they have to hang around to digest everything before they can begin to think about flying off.

Having acclimatised in Lhasa, it is time to leave. Wherever you are heading, it is a long drive. Land Cruisers are the vehicle of choice as they are extremely good at off-road journeys. They do break down, however, and journeys can take a lot longer than expected. The drivers used to have a reputation for being truculent and unhelpful, but with increased competition they have had to improve their service. They are a resilient bunch when it comes to breaking down. There is no roadside service and very few places where repairs could be carried out. There have been several occasions on my journeys when the bonnet has needed to be lifted or the vehicle to be jacked up. The most worrying occasion was when the leaf spring suspension broke on our vehicle. Usually, that is pretty catastrophic, and when I saw it I thought we would be at the roadside for a long time. The solution was simple. The driver took off his trouser belt, coiled it around the broken springs and buckled it tightly. Remarkably, it worked, and lasted for the remainder of the time we were using the vehicle but I'm not sure how he kept his trousers up!

The journey provides some stunning "top of the pass" views, in particular the 5150m Pang La, which gives stunning views of the northern side of the Himalayan range. Standing proud above all other peaks is Everest. Whenever we stopped for a view, we would not be able to see a soul for miles. Then, we would see people running towards us, desperate to get to us before we climbed back into out vehicles. Most of them would turn out to be dirty, spiky-haired children, who would wander among us, from one to another, hoping that we would have something to give them.

At one place, lower down, we stopped for lunch in the middle of nowhere. Soon curious children surrounded us. It can be uncomfortable sitting eating in front of children who might well be hungry. Time to entertain them. We were carrying some long balloons, which squeaked when released. Children love chasing them. While I and one or two others were keeping them entertained, the ladies among us decided to sneak off for a private moment in some bushes. It was quiet, until one of the balloons went off course, into the bushes, chased by a dozen or so children! There is no such thing as privacy in Tibet.

At one village we visited en route to Everest, there were loudspeakers pointing in the four compass points, constantly blaring out Chinese music and propaganda. Considering this was a totally Tibetan village, apart from one or two Chinese officials, it seemed strange. When I enquired about it, I was told it was to motivate the people to work harder.

The title of truculent and unhelpful now belongs to the yak men who carry all the trekking equipment and our personal kit. Their timekeeping is appalling, being late to arrive on many occasions, sometimes by hours rather than minutes.

Also, if they don't want to go somewhere, they make it very clear. In 2007 we were hoping to trek up the Kangshun Valley to the little-visited Kangshun face on the east side of Everest. We soon hit snow, not vast amounts but enough to make it a more interesting walk. We picked our route carefully and were never in any difficulty. The yaks, we were led to believe, were finding it difficult; they were in danger of breaking a leg on the rocks under the surface of the snow. I found this hard to believe. This is where yaks live all the time. The yak men were having none of it and we had to turn back and rethink our trek.

In the event of not going to the Kangshun face, we trekked

around to the north side of Everest and the Rongbuk Valley, where base camp is situated. It was an extremely cold trek.

On the two occasions I have been to Rongbuk I have camped near the monastery, a most incredible location with views of Everest. It looks very different according to the season. I first went there during July, when Nepal is affected by the monsoon rains. Some of those rains manage to reach the northern side of the Himalayas, ensuring that Everest has a good coating of fresh snow. We were very lucky on that occasion, for Everest was cloud free all the time we were there.

In April, there is far less snow and a lot more rock showing.

Whenever you are there it is an awesome sight, in many ways so much better than the views you get on the Nepal side. Here, you can see the whole mountain, whereas in Nepal there are too many other mountains in the way.

From camp it is a five-mile walk up the valley to base camp. Westerners cannot drive up, fortunately, but you can take a pony and trap, if so desired. Chinese can drive up to the end of the road. It is a great walk, always with the northern wall of Everest to look at. It only disappoints when you reach a few shacks near the end, selling really tatty souvenirs, or offering unthinkable accommodation. One shack is called Hotel California!

Just beyond the eyesore is a mound covered in prayer flags. Climbing to the top of that, you get a view of the whole of Everest. In the foreground is the outflow from the Rongbuk Glacier and base camp. Beyond is the entrance to the East Rongbuk Glacier and the northern route to the summit. It is quite an emotional experience to sit on this mound, looking at Everest. It proved to be an ideal spot for taking a moment to reflect on life.

Of course, the whole mood can be spoilt. While I was there in 2004, a Land Cruiser arrived, disgorging its passenger, a smartly dressed Chinese woman with a skirt, coat and heeled patent shoes. She carefully picked her way to the top of the mound, careful not to scuff her shoes, took a "selfie" with Everest in the background, tottered back down the slope, climbed into the Land Cruiser and drove back to wherever she came!

In order to get back to Nepal, we drive west, parallel to the Himalayas as far as Nyalam, which translates to "the gateway to hell". Wrong: it is hell! I prefer to describe Nyalam as the "groin of the world". There has been a significant building project in the town, but nothing has been finished and it is all turning into an eyesore.

The local population seem to be poorer here than anywhere I have seen in Tibet. The men have nothing to do and seem to spend the day drinking, while the downtrodden women look after starving children, picking nits from their hair. There had been many joyous moments in Tibet but this was turning out to be a very depressing finale.

Even the Chinese looked depressed, as if this were the last outpost to which anybody would want to be sent. We understood that many criminals were being sent to this area, and other remote areas, to work on the roads. Tibet was rapidly becoming a penal colony.

Even we had nothing to do, nowhere to go.

It was with a great deal of relief that we only spent one night in Nyalam, and we were happy to be back on the road to Nepal. It was a bad night. There was drunkenness in the street below. Dogs barked continuously. In the middle of the night our peace was further disturbed by the arrival of more drunks, who relieved themselves against our bedroom doors!

It was with a great deal of relief that we climbed into our Land Cruisers for the last leg of out Tibetan journey.

A short distance out of Nyalam the atmosphere lifted and the scenery became spectacular as we headed towards the Bhot Khosi Gorge. The river was a raging, deafening torrent. By now the road was nothing more than a dirt track. As it entered the gorge it became a single-track shelf, high up on the side of the cliff. Sitting on the right of the Land Cruiser gave us vertiginous views down to the turbulent waters below. One mistake, one error of judgement on the part of our driver, would be certain death. Waterfalls tumbled over us and at one point the driver stopped under one to wash his vehicle. It is one of the great road journeys of the world.

At the end of the gorge there is a bridge across the river. This marks the border. Before we reach the bridge we have to say farewell to our Land Cruiser drivers and walk the last few metres into Nepal. Across the centre of the bridge there is a red line, marking the exact boundary. It is customary to straddle the line with one foot in Tibet and the other in Nepal.

Would I go to Tibet again? Yes. There is so much more to see. I don't like supporting repressive regimes but I always have in the back of my mind something that a Tibetan said to me: "Don't stop coming to Tibet because of the Chinese. If you don't come, we will be forgotten and lost forever." Tibet is not perfect. Tibetans are not perfect, although some of that can be attributed to the way they have been treated. Tibetans add a richness to this world and it would be a great shame if the world forgot them.

17

—

THE NORTH SIDE OF K2

While I enjoy visiting old haunts, particularly Nepal, it is inspiring to visit new cultures, new countries and new outstanding mountains. In the spring of 2012 a group of us embarked on a journey that was to be a real eye-opener in so many ways. We were heading for the north side of K2 on the China/Pakistan border, but starting our journey in Bishkek, Kyrgyzstan, some 700 miles to the north. It was a journey full of interest, both culturally and geographically.

Bishkek is built on a grid system, so is quite easy to get around. The roads are wide and tree-lined. The trees help to hide our view of large Russian housing blocks looking bleak and run-down. I soon realised I was seeing Bishkek at just about the worst time of year. Nature was still asleep after the winter, but the snow had gone, leaving everywhere looking bland, grey and uninteresting. I would not describe Bishkek as dirty, though. People were out in front of their houses and shops sweeping, clearing up the autumn leaves and making things look tidy. There is very little litter at the sides of the roads. Exploring the city it soon became clear that there are large areas of parkland available for public use. Throughout the city there are irrigation pipes to water the grass and flowers during the relatively brief but hot, dry summer.

Walking around Bishkek, I had the feeling it is a reluctant capital city. It is quiet. Any noise is quite muted. It has not been overwhelmed with consumerism; shops do not stand out and hit you in the face but are hidden behind fairly dull facades, almost embarrassed to show themselves. Perhaps people do not have the money to spend and I am not sure what people do to earn a living. When the Soviet Union lost control, many of the Soviet factories closed down and remain, today, as a derelict symbol of the past. Other factories have fallen into decline because they were owned by friends of the first president, who was ousted by the people during the Tulip Revolution in 2005. Taxis line the streets but nobody seems to use them so taxi drivers hang around waiting for custom, looking bored and dejected.

On either side of the main street, Chui Avenue, there are some large, solid buildings left over from the Russian era. They cannot be described as beautiful but are imposing monuments to power over people. In front of these buildings are dramatic statues depicting heroic struggle.

We left Bishkek and started our journey towards the Chinese border. The road followed the Ushi River, which forms the border between Kyrgyzstan and Kazakhstan. A razor wire fence and lookout towers decorate the other side of the river.

We stopped in the village of Kochkor for lunch, not in a restaurant but in a home stay. The house was immaculate inside and, remarkably, all of us were able to sit around one table, heaving with food: not just the meal but also the accompaniments. The first course was a plate of salad with a fennel dressing. This was followed by noodle soup with potato and pieces of tender lamb. Thinking that was it, you can imagine our surprise to receive a plate of beef, rice, buckwheat and vegetables.

The post-lunch journey saw us climbing further until we reached the top of the 3030m Dolon Pass. Deep snow lay all around us. From the pass it was downhill to Naryn, a former Russian military town, which now seems to have little going for it. Until the Russians left, it was a "no go" area as it had military significance and things were happening here that they did not want the rest of the world to know about.

The next day was a day of snow and checkpoints. We left Naryn and climbed out of the valley to the appropriately named Red Pass. This led onto a wide, high plateau with a mountain chain on either side. Here the snow was deep in places, piled high on either side of the road. It was cold and bleak.

At our first checkpoint we could stay in the vehicles but our Kyrgyz guide had to take our passports to be scrutinised. This done, we continued towards the border. We soon came across a stationary convoy of lorries blocking our way. The front bus, driven by Vladimir, known as "Vlad the Impaler", took the cavalier approach by attempting to drive past the convoy, where there was clearly not enough room. Sure enough, the front of the bus plunged off the road and into deep snow, leaving us leaning precariously to one side. Thankfully, the second minibus did not attempt to follow.

In his haste, Vlad managed to dig the bus deeper into the snow. Our second bus positioned itself to attach a tow strap but it did not have the power for the job. With thirteen English, Vlad, Mikael, and an assortment of Kyrgyzstani and Chinese lorry drivers all chipping in with ideas, we did not get very far, particularly as everything the English suggested was ignored. The line was now attached to the front of a lorry but with the front wheels firmly entrenched it was not long before the line snapped. The simple solution was to dig out the snow behind the front wheels but it was hard to get the message across and nobody understood what we meant. The now shortened line snapped again, as did the steel wire used next. Eventually we found a shovel and cleared the snow. The combined strap and steel wire then did the job and the bus was pulled free and back onto the road.

Before we went any further, snow chains were fitted to our vehicles, while the lorries obligingly moved over enough to give us room to pass.

Next stop was at the Kyrgyzstan border post, where we had to leave our vehicles and go into a fridge of a building. The marble floor had a layer of ice on top, making it lethal. We queued up to have our exit stamps, which took a while, and by the time that was done we all needed the loo. Unfortunately, the loo was on the Kyrgyzstan side and we were now on the Chinese side and could not go back!

We had now entered "no man's land". The snow on the top of the pass was several feet deep and despite the sunshine there was a cold breeze. Our bus was not able to reach us, being stuck behind lorries, so we set off to walk down the road to meet it. The scenery was stunning with white, snow-clad mountains as far as the eye could see. It was good to stretch our legs.

We discovered that we were the first tourists this year to cross into China via the Torugart Pass. The scenery on the Chinese side of the pass suddenly became even more spectacular. The other side was beautiful but it had a bleakness about it, and lacked the "wow" factor. This side had everything: vertical faces, pointed peaks and snowfields. Beautiful!

A hundred kilometres inside China, we came to the customs post, where we had to have our entry stamped and our bags checked. This was the bit I was worried about because we were carrying a lot of cash but I should not have bothered. As we lined up we had our temperatures taken. Anybody born after 1978 had to have a polio vaccination. Two of our group fell into that category but they refused to have it, so had to sign a disclaimer.

An hour later we were in Kashgar. We had been on the road, stuck in snow or having our passports checked for thirteen hours.

We stayed in the Tianyuan International Hotel. It is right in the centre of town, adjacent to the People's Square, lit up lavishly at night and overlooked by a giant statue of Mao. The hotel is comfortable and clean but has some features that cause amusement and intrigue. In the bathroom of each room there was a basket, by the washbowl, which contained a variety of products. I don't think I have stayed in a hotel before where such products are so readily available – condoms, arousal oils and creams for "him" and "her" with very clear instructions as to which part of the anatomy they should be applied to, and for how long, and cream to prevent premature ejaculation. Nothing was left to the imagination.

Kashgar is a bustling, vibrant city. As we walked about the streets we took our lives into our hands. Nearly everybody had an electric scooter, which was fantastic for keeping the city's noise levels down but also meant we did not hear them as they aimed straight for us from behind. It is necessary to have your wits about you at all times, even if you think you are safe on the pavement – scooters can, and do, go everywhere.

We focused our attention on the older and more interesting Uyghur area of city, calling first at Cotton Traders Road. This road might have been known for cotton trading in the past but now it holds a variety of handicraft shops, which seem to bunch together according to craft skills. The first group we came across were copper and tin workers who created vessels of every size and shape and then hammer them to give them texture. There were jewellery shops, bread shops, carpet shops, hat shops, wooden crafts and musical instrument shops.

Around the corner we visited the yellow-tiled Idkah Mosque before going on to the old town, built on a hill of dried mud. The majority of the houses were made of wattle and daub, although some were being replaced using more modern materials.

We visited the Aba Khoja Mausoleum, the final resting place of the Fragrant Concubine, Xiangfei. There were casks from five generations in the mausoleum, which, with their colourful silk drapes, would have made an interesting picture, had photos been allowed.

Finally we went to the Sunday Market (open every day but called that as Sunday is the main market day), where there was an array of things on sale from shoes to materials, from nuts to stockings, from electrical goods to toys. I was hijacked from my wanderings to speak to a young man running a pashmina and scarf stall. He did not want to sell me anything but just wanted to improve his English. We were joined by a couple of his mates, who did not speak English, and the questions flowed. It was an enjoyable way of spending twenty minutes.

Observing the comings and goings through the hotel reception as we returned from our evening out, I came to the conclusion that the hotel was a rather expensive knocking shop for businessmen. There was a nightclub on the fifth floor where businessmen picked up young girls, took them to their rooms and made use of the facilities and products on offer, so long as, according to the rules, visitors were gone by 1.00am.

After a leisurely breakfast we vacated our rooms and boarded our Land Cruisers for the journey to Kargilik (Yecheng). It gave us an opportunity to see the extent of growth and development of Kashgar, with massive housing projects on a scale unprecedented in the UK. The speed and scale of development was phenomenal.

The landscape throughout the journey was flat. I doubt there was a fluctuation in height more than 10m all day. To begin with, once we had left the urbanisation of the city, we passed farmland composed of small fields. The road was brilliant, brand new and in places cut right through the middle of these farming communities, not providing them with anything but destroying their community and environment. Where there wasn't farmland, there was a barren, stony, infertile wasteland, the Taklamakan Desert, the second largest desert in the world. Gradually, white, snow-capped peaks came into view on our right, although we did not venture much towards them but ran parallel with them. The further we went, the more barren the landscape became. We stopped at a "services". I use the term loosely as it was nothing more than a flattened area of desert awaiting development. Soon, a railway ran parallel to the motorway, linking Kashgar to cities 5000km away on the other side of China. These new transport communications help speed up the colonisation of the west by people from the east, given financial incentives from the government. It is so easy for the Chinese to move huge numbers to the west and swamp the indigenous Muslim population. It is hardly surprising that the Uyghurs are unhappy and feel the need to make their feelings known from time to time. Hence the need for the Chinese to make their presence felt with SWAT teams and over-zealous police surveillance. I think the Chinese philosophy of "progress at any cost" was summed up when the motorway we were travelling on scythed through the middle of a cemetery with no regard for the feelings such action might produce.

Every so often we would see a station on the parallel railway line, but it was a station in the middle of nowhere. Then we would notice lots of white marker posts hammered into the barren earth, just poking above the surface. These markers showed where roads would go and where buildings would rise, creating the next town to aid the colonisation of this region.

On reaching Yecheng, our vehicle took us to the strangely named Electricity Hotel. Having disembarked, our driver received a call to say we had to go to the police post to have our passports registered. This took quite a while as our names were carefully written into a register. Job done, we returned to the Electricity Hotel. It was not very clean. The walls had damp and peeling wallpaper and there was a musty smell about the place. One room had dried vomit down the wall adjacent to the bed. Most people rearranged the furniture to avoid coming into contact with anything unsavoury and, just in case the beds were infested, many of us used our sleeping bags.

We decided to go for a walk and explore the town, which was much bigger than imagined. We noticed a lot of soldiers and police on the street corners as we drove around and were warned not to go too far from the hotel as a couple of weeks previously there had been a bomb, hence the military presence. It was not unpleasant walking around, although it was as though the circus had come to town and we were it! We were the only white faces in town and we appealed to the children coming out of school. We also appealed to a member of the Chinese Secret Police, whom we spotted following us. He was wearing a brown leather jacket and kept speaking into his lapel. There were five in our little group and when we got together with others we discovered that they too had been followed and, in each case, the followers were wearing brown leather jackets and had been talking into their lapels!

We left Yecheng and drove south across the desert, eventually reaching the foothills. Now we steadily climbed up a series of hairpin bends to the 3150m summit of a mountain pass. The view over the other side was superb, with a huge wall of snow-capped mountains on the horizon and orange, brown and red mountains in the foreground. From the pass the road dropped dramatically to the valley floor below to follow the Kudi River.

Soon the good road turned into a "work in progress", which slowed us slightly. We eventually reached the top of the next pass at about 4900m.

Eventually we reached the village of Mazar, which is nothing more than a junction with a few shoddily built shacks. If you turned left you followed the iron ore trucks, or right you followed the Yarkand River to Yilik, where there was another checkpoint. Having successfully passed through the checkpoint we travelled a few more kilometres to the village of Yilik and our first camp. It had been a fantastic if rather long journey and, because our arrival was quite late, some of the group were able to sleep in a village house, while the rest of us pitched tents nearby. It was a beautiful, if chilly, starlit night.

Once the camels arrived the next morning, we were able to set off on the trek. Despite the fact that it was a good path and any gradients were easy, it was still a bit of a struggle. First days often are and, after a week of travelling in vehicles, walking at 3500m is always going to be difficult. Having come over the shoulder at the end of a ridge separating the valley with Yilik and the Yarkand River, the walk became more interesting. The river-cut valley was fabulous, with a braided river on the flat bed and steep cliffs on either side. Looking up towards the head of the valley, there were beautiful snow-capped peaks.

Another point of interest lay on the riverbed, where there were huge lumps of jade. One rock, Hira estimated, would be worth about

£1,000,000! Having found one, we found lots. It is hard to imagine that the Chinese have not taken advantage of such a treasure at their feet. Obviously, iron ore is more precious to them.

The following morning we continued up the gorge, with spectacular cliffs on either side, with hardly any sign of vegetation.

It is very difficult to judge distances in this environment. We could see our target along the valley, or the next bend or rocky outcrop, but it took ages to reach. In places the riverbed might be a mile or more across, with mountains rising vertically on either side for several thousand feet.

We set about the task of climbing and crossing the Aghil Pass. It was expected that it would take us about five hours to reach the top. With the wind blowing fiercely in our faces, it actually took about five and a half hours. It was stunningly beautiful, with rocky, snowy mountains to either side. We alternated between walking on stony paths and snowfields. On one of the snowfields we came across the pawprints of snow leopards, two adults and a young one.

I had hoped to have lunch on the top and admire the view. It gave a superb panoramic view of the Karakorum Mountains to the south, with Gasherbrum 2 and 3 being the most spectacular. Unfortunately, it was too windy and there was nowhere to shelter. It was disappointing that the conditions did not allow for us to linger. Instead, we focused our attention on getting down out of the wind.

The path down was good and as I was walking on my own I was able to make good progress. The lower I got, however, the more complicated it became. There was no sign of a clear path and it was simply a case of picking my way through a boulder field. Eventually, I had a choice to make. The riverbed descended into a gorge with steep cliffs on either side. Should I follow that or stay above it? We were directed into the gorge as it was a short cut, avoiding a three-hour detour, which the camels had to make. The riverbed in the gorge was strewn with huge boulders and the cliffs looked very dangerous, with rocks defying gravity and clinging to the loose material in-between. Sometimes we had to scramble down dry waterfalls, making our descent more interesting. All the time we could hear rockfalls on the slopes above and it felt as if it were only a matter of time before boulders would come crashing down into the gorge.

Eventually we emerged into the magnificent Shagskam River valley, with mountains towering above. Here the river was about a mile across and it seemed to take ages to pick our way across it to our camp on the other side. It was a super spot for camping among some low bushes with a spring emerging from the rock wall adjacent to the camp.

The whole of the next day was spent walking along the Shagskam riverbed across a mixture of stones and large areas of frozen river. It was much easier walking on the ice as the stones proved very tiring on the feet. It seemed to go on forever and while we were walking we had to concentrate on our feet and not take in the beautiful scenery around us.

We reached camp late in the afternoon and pitched our tents in the strong breeze, which seemed to be a feature of each afternoon.

The next morning we continued along the river to the junction with the Sarpo Largo River, where we climbed up onto a shoulder above for our first view of K2. By the time we got to the viewpoint, the cloud had begun to build up and, although the outline was visible, it was not very clear. The mountains around it were pretty spectacular but K2 stood out head and shoulders above them.

Dropping back down to the river we continued towards Chinese Base Camp. Along the way we had to cross the frozen K2 River. On the frozen river lay the corpse of a kiang, a wild ass, which had fallen victim to a snow leopard, the stomach and the heart being the only meat taken.

Chinese Base Camp, at 3900m, proved to be a very cold place at night.

Trekking up to Chinese Base Camp was fantastic. One of the things, I think, that makes it very special is its remoteness. When Shipton explored this area he wrote the book *Blank on the Map*. That is exactly what this is. There are no villages, no people; we were the only ones there with nobody else in the world within at least thirty-five miles in any direction.

Our first day above Chinese Base Camp took us as far as Pakistan Base Camp at the snout of the glacier. It was lovely to be walking on a proper mountain path as we climbed out of camp. The path took us to a pass and a traverse around a spur into the K2 valley. We were surrounded by stunning peaks. As yet, the elusive K2 had not shown herself.

In order to reach Pakistan Base Camp we had to descend into the valley via a loose soil path down a very steep slope, a remnant of when the glacier had reached this far down the valley. The only ice now was the frozen K2 River and we could see the snout of the glacier just beyond our camp. As we got closer to camp, and the glacier, the air cooled significantly. Camp was a dry platform on the edge of the very fragile cliff down to the river. As we arrived the crew were collecting water in a barrel, having first made a hole in the ice to get at the water below. The barrel was then hauled up the cliff with a rope.

As the afternoon progressed into evening, the clouds cleared from K2, giving us some superb photographic shots in the evening light.

The night proved not to be quite as cold as expected for cloud rolled in and dumped a couple of inches of snow on us. It was still snowing, although only lightly, when we emerged from our tents for breakfast. The sun soon forced its way through the cloud and we were able to proceed to Italian Base Camp, several kilometres up the glacier and a few hundred metres higher at around 4800m.

Our journey took us through an area of extremely fragile landscape, which brought imminent danger from rockfall, landslide and possible avalanche. We were having to watch constantly where we put our feet on the rocky, stony surface searching for a hardly discernible path. All we could do was link a series of small cairns (only two or three stones in height) to be sure we were on the right track. After seven ankle-twisting, foot-bruising hours we reached Italian Base Camp. It is situated at the side of the glacier in a very barren, rocky landscape. A few relatively stone-free platforms have been created for tents. Despite its barrenness it was a most amazing place.

Now that we were in camp at 4700m, we could take in the scenery around us. Further up the valley, head and shoulders above anything, was the beautiful and spellbinding K2. On either side it was flanked by lesser, but nonetheless beautiful, peaks. Descending from the foot of K2 snaked the glacier, in the main covered with rocky debris, out of which soared pure white pinnacles of ice. Other glaciers tumbled from smaller side valleys to interfere with the downward flow of the main glacier. This place is special.

The following morning we could choose what we wanted to do. We were not going to camp any nearer to K2. The terrain was much too difficult for the donkeys and camel men to carry the kit and suitable camping places were minimal. Also, the further up the glacier we went the more technical the journey would become. Going from Italian Base Camp, we could explore further up the glacier.

One group went with one of the camel drivers as a guide to get a closer look at the awesome pinnacles on the glacier. Others, including me, preferred just to potter about on the glacier and enjoy its features and those of the surrounding peaks. The ice sculpturing brought about by opposing pressures was fantastic. We ambled up to a point where a hanging glacier tumbled into the main glacier. Here there was more activity, with occasional icefalls entertaining us. We sat in very pleasant sunshine for some considerable time chatting while, all the time, taking in the scenery.

The following morning was particularly cold, with an in-tent temperature of –15°C recorded. The outside temperature would have been a few degrees lower. Our breath had condensed on the walls of the tents and turned to frost.

We were given the freedom to head down as soon as we were ready, rather than wait for our guides. As we descended, wisps of cloud, like fingers, encircled K2. She had revealed herself to us throughout our time at the high camps. Now that we were leaving, she was covering herself up again as a sign of farewell.

The journey down to Pakistan Base Camp took four hours and although faster than our ascent it required maximum concentration.

From Pakistan Base Camp we had to climb up the steep, precarious path out of the valley and from there on it was a delightful romp back to Chinese Base Camp. The weather seemed to be deteriorating so those of us who made it to camp first put up all the tents.

Before we left Chinese Base Camp we discussed whether we wanted a rest day, before going back over the Aghil Pass, or to continue through without a rest day and have an extra day in Kashgar. Surprisingly, everybody preferred to finish early and have the extra day in a hotel. As it turned out, this was the best decision.

Given the freedom to leave camp when we were ready, before the crew were properly organised, we set off, retracing our steps. I don't enjoy this aspect of linear treks and prefer circular routes, so I put my head down and strode out. When we came to the K2 River we approached cautiously, in case there were any visitors to the dead kiang on the ice. There were none, but it was interesting to note that in the time we had been on the mountain the level of the ice had dropped about a foot, except where the kiang lay, which was now raised on an ice plinth.

Along the Shagskam River there had been a noticeable reduction in the ice and we were faced with a number of river crossings during the afternoon, where only a few days previously we had been able to cross on the ice. Fortunately, the river was never more than knee deep where we chose to cross. I don't think I would have wanted it much deeper as it was still extremely cold. As it was, our feet felt very refreshed and had a much-needed wash!

Later in the afternoon, just before we reached camp, there was one final river crossing. For this, the camels came back to carry everyone. I chose not to take advantage of the camels but to walk through the river as I was already wearing my water shoes, and I wanted to be in a position to film the crossing. I am so pleased I took that decision. David had grown very fond of a particular camel, a blond, leggy specimen with long fluttery eyelashes. He eagerly climbed aboard and Robin joined him on the back of the animal. The camel had a fiery personality and bucked from side to side, causing both David and Robin to hang on for dear life. I have never seen David look so frightened.

David and Robin got off lightly, however, compared with Simon and Chris, who rode their placid-natured camel with confidence. That was until the camel started to climb up the bank, having crossed safely. Its legs gave way and then it began to slide back down the bank, into the river, dumping Simon into the water, giving him wet feet and, more worryingly, wet boots. Chris managed to save himself and maintained his dignity.

The weather was now not as clear or as bright as it had been on the way up and it was not getting any warmer.

We were now at the foot of the Aghil Pass and we had two to three inches of snow and it was still falling. The flakes were incredibly fine and it was a dry snow but we knew it might be a different story the higher we climbed.

Setting off, we first had to cross the mile-wide riverbed to the mouth of the gorge. It was a steady climb up the boulder-strewn gorge bed, with the occasional scramble up the still dry waterfalls. We kept a wary eye on the cliffs above just in case a boulder should free itself from its fragile sandy bed. We kept the noise down to a minimum, just in case sound should dislodge a rock. Also, temperature rises can affect the stability of such fragile landscapes so we wanted to pass through this area as quickly as we could. Forty-five minutes saw us scrambling out of the gorge and the danger had passed.

We now had to pick our route through a maze of rocks and gullies towards the pass. With height gained, the snow deepened and some began to feel less comfortable. It was clear they were being affected by the cold and altitude. I took the initiative to lead by doing the "Walton plod". On the other side of the pass the wind was in our faces. This meant that there was much more snow gathered on our downward slope and for much of the time it was knee deep, with many hidden dips and tussocks for us to twist an ankle.

Taking time for the camels to catch up and overtake, we paused for lunch. My beard was a frozen mass of icicles. The camels, now ahead of us, paved the way, flattening the snow and making walking much easier and safer. It was a long descent, about three hours, and just before camp I caught up with the camels. I was intrigued by how quiet and placid they were. They required no instruction or encouragement; they just plodded on their dinner-plate-sized feet, flattening the snow for me to follow. It was the same when they reached camp. A little click of the tongue instructed them to sit so they could be unloaded and a second click told them to stand again.

As we arrived in camp it started to snow more heavily, making the putting up of tents a miserable affair. Once up, we snuggled down to keep warm. We did not bother with the mess tent and our food was brought to us.

It snowed all night. When we woke up we realised just what a good decision it had been not to take an offered rest day before the Aghil Pass. Had we done so we would not have been able to cross, the snow would have been getting on for waist deep, and, while we might have been able to exhaustingly plough our way through, the camels and donkeys would not.

As we moved further down the valley the snow lessened so that by the time we reached camp it had all gone, not melted but evaporated, leaving the ground as dry as it had been before any snow had fallen.

In the morning more snow had fallen, but it did not last long as the sun soon cleared it away. We only had to walk the short distance to Yilik, estimated to be about four hours. In fact, it only took some of us three hours as we put our heads down and got on with the job. Once we entered the Yilik Valley we were faced with a strong, cold wind but, after what seemed an endless trudge to the village, we reached the shelter of the house that was hosting us.

When we had left Yilik two weeks previously there were signs that some building work was going to take place a short distance from the village. On our return a crane was in place and the shells of several buildings had been erected. This is all part of the Chinese policy of rehousing communities out of their mud-constructed houses and into more modern, but less individualistic houses.

When everybody finally arrived at Yilik we all had an opportunity to ride the camels briefly. David, determined to make amends for his girly screaming three days previously, girded his loins and mounted Blondie. She was far more accepting this time.

After a night in Yilik, we packed everything in our Land Cruisers and began the long journey to Bishkek. Although we were, largely, retracing our steps, there were aspects of the journey that were very different. For a start, the yet-to-be-built motorway services we had stopped at on the outward journey were built and fully functioning.

Back in the hotel in Kashgar, some of us chose to visit the KTV floor, affectionately known among us as the KY Jelly Bar. We had been warned to stay away as it was not suitable for us. It's a bit like telling a child not to do something.

Emerging from the lift on the fifth floor, I went in search of the bar. There were lots of mirrors, coloured lighting and wailing voices. When I asked where the bar was, we were led along a corridor past rooms full of people making lots of noise and into a room of our own. The room consisted of a long couch, a coffee table, a large-screen TV and a computer. Drinks were brought in, along with two microphones. The TV and computer were switched on and the 1960s and '70s music began to play. The wailing we had heard before was from people trying to sing their favourite songs. We had a bizarre selection, from the Carpenters to "Yellow Submarine" and we soon discovered that we could wail as well as the next room. Beers drunk, we were told we could have three more without extra cost; presumably we had paid for the room and a certain number of beers. While it was fun initially, the novelty wore off quite quickly.

After a couple of days in Kashgar, we hit the road again, climbing up to the border at the Torugart Pass. Simon and Rob were really very ill, having eaten some street food. It was going to be a very difficult journey for them.

In the main the slopes were clear of snow, certainly on the lower hills, and the rivers were running with orange water, a sure sign that spring was on its way in these hills. There was much less snow and hardly a lorry in sight as we approached the top of the Torugart Pass and the actual border.

Without the snow, the road was unmade and uneven, making the journey to Naryn a long, bone-rattling affair. Bring back the snow! The high-altitude plateau was now alive with life. Where three weeks ago there had been a white scape, there were now herds of horses, cattle and flocks of sheep and goats grazing and tended to by farmers on horseback. Woken from their winter sleep, marmots gambolled in the warm sunshine. It was an idyllic scene, always with the backdrop of snow-capped mountains.

Leaving Naryn, we crossed one more pass before we started our descent to the plains below. We took a slight detour on the journey to visit Lake Isyk-Kol, a huge expanse of water (the second largest mountain lake in the world after Titicaca), where the Russians had had a torpedo factory and carried out tests on the lake. Typical of most industrial sites in Kyrgyzstan, it now lies derelict and testimony to a past under Russian control. The situation of the lake is superb with snow-capped mountains all around. It has a much better future as a tourist destination, once the economy can allow investment.

The final leg of our journey took us to Bishkek. The sunshine was warm, leaves out on the trees, fruit trees in blossom, men fishing in the river and couples picnicking on the riverbank. It was such a different picture to the one we had seen only three weeks previously. In just three weeks Kyrgyzstan had been transported from winter to summer.

In Bishkek, the tree-lined streets were green, people wore summer clothes and the hotel garden was bathed in the perfume of lilac. Bishkek looked a lot more attractive.

Kyrgyzstan had opened my eyes to many exciting possibilities and I was grateful to return twice with expeditions in the years that followed.

18

—

A RELAXING MASSAGE IN KASHGAR

It had been a long trip. Having started in Bishkek, Kyrgyzstan, we had driven for four days, over the Torugart Pass into China, across the Taklamakan Desert to the start of the trek. The trek, in a really remote corner of the world, took us through some of the most dramatic scenery imaginable to the north side of the magnificent K2.

By the time we reached Kashgar on the return journey, still with two more days on the road ahead of us, my body ached. I thought I would take advantage of the spa at the Tianyuan International Hotel, a modern, well-appointed hotel adjacent to the People's Park with a sixty-foot statue of Chairman Mao overlooking it.

Going up to the reception, I asked, "Could I book a massage in the spa, please?"

The smiling receptionist replied, "Sorry, sir, spa is closed."

"When will it be opening?" I asked, hopefully.

"Not opening. Closed for decorating," replied my smiling receptionist.

Disappointed, I asked, "Are there any other hotels similar to this, where I can get a massage?"

"Ah, yes," he said, tearing off a street map of Kashgar from the pad on the reception desk. "This hotel give good massage," he said, drawing a circle around its location on the map.

It looked as if it was the other side of town. "How far?" I asked.

"Five minutes in taxi. I call you a taxi?"

"Er, yes please," I said tentatively, beginning to wonder what I was letting myself in for. "Will they understand me?"

"I write down, on piece of paper, what you want." With that he wrote down a few lines of Chinese script, which, as far as I was concerned, could have said anything.

Handing me the piece of paper, he came out from behind reception, past the riot squad sitting in the lounge area next to the large windows, to the doors through which we passed to flag down a taxi and give the driver instructions.

Before I get into the taxi, I feel I ought to explain the riot squad. The indigenous population of this part of China are the Uyghurs, who are Muslim and look more like Turks than Chinese. The Ottoman Empire stretched this far east, so it is hardly surprising. The Chinese are relative newcomers to this region, gradually spreading their power and influence as they flex their muscles, expanding their empire. Unfortunately, in order to maintain their control, they have to keep the indigenous population under close scrutiny and exert strength over them. Occasionally this requires soldiers to go and beat a few Uyghurs to maintain their control through fear. The dozen or so soldiers billeted in the lounge area, watching from behind net curtains, would don full riot gear, go out and beat a few Uyghurs up before returning to the hotel for coffee.

It struck me as being very sinister and unsavoury treatment of a people whose main concern was earning enough to put food on the table. Of course, the situation has deteriorated much more for the Uyghurs since I was there in 2012.

As I climbed into the taxi the receptionist told the driver where to take me. It seemed that we were going along the main street to the other side of town. It is quite an interesting street in as much as on one side there are high-rise shopping malls and hotels, displaying rampant commercialism. White goods were stacked ten high on the pavement. On the other side of the street it was more Third World, where the Uyghurs traded in small-fronted, low-level, basic shops. The contrast was remarkable.

The taxi pulled up outside a hotel and the driver told me that this was my destination. He didn't exactly say that. He said, "You go now. In there." Paying my fare, I exited the taxi and went through the large double doors into the reception area of the hotel.

Clutching my piece of paper, I nervously went up to reception, behind which were three young people, two young men and a girl.

"I would like a massage," I said.

They looked at me blankly, and then at each other.

"Do you speak English?" I asked.

They shook their heads. This was the cue for me to hand over the piece of paper.

They looked at it but, worryingly, there was not a flicker of understanding being displayed on their faces.

After a moment, they showed me the room tariff sheet, with photos of the rooms and the cost of each.

"No, no, I don't want a room, I want a massage," I explained, rubbing one hand over the other arm and shoulder, in the hope that a visual display would bring about their understanding.

Again, they looked at each other. "You don't want room?" one said tentatively.

So they can speak a little English.

"No, no, I want massage in spa." It suddenly occurred to me that if I used the word spa it might generate a glimmer of understanding. But it didn't. I was getting nowhere fast and I was about to give up, to walk out into the street, when a voice behind me said, "Can I help?"

Ah, brilliant, someone who can speak English. I turned to face the voice and standing there was a short, middle-aged Chinese woman in a dark dress.

"Yes, please," I said, "I am trying to book a massage in the spa."

Her blank expression suggested she didn't understand. Perhaps,

"Can I help?" was the limit of her English. This isn't getting me very far, very fast. I showed her the piece of paper my receptionist had given me. This prompted a conversation between the three receptionists and my potential saviour, which resulted in me being told to go to the fifth floor.

At last, I was getting somewhere.

Great ceremony was made of putting me into the lift and the appropriate button being pressed to get me up to the fifth floor. I was soon heading up five floors on a journey into the unknown.

With a ping the lift stopped and the doors opened. Standing there to greet me were four young people, all dressed in hotel uniform. They ushered me out to the small reception area for the spa.

"I would like a massage, please," I said optimistically.

That produced much giggling and chatter but no instruction. The look on their faces suggested that they really didn't know what I wanted. This was beginning to prove very stressful and, if I hadn't needed a massage before, I certainly needed one now.

Without coming to any conclusions as to what I wanted, they ushered me into a room and left me alone. There was a massage bed at least, so maybe they understood.

I waited a few moments. The door opened and in walked someone I was not expecting and who put me in some fear and trepidation. He was a young man who I could probably best describe as chunky! He was wearing a thick, blue tracksuit and blue wellingtons! I couldn't help noticing that his hands were the size of dinner plates! What have I let myself in for? I could die here, and nobody would know.

"Massage?" he asked.

"Yes, please," I stammered.

Pointing at the clock and circling his finger 360°, he said, "One hour. Sixty yuan."

I nodded my head and fumbled for my wallet. I handed him his sixty yuan, equivalent to about £8.

He thrust a silk two-piece outfit into my hand and said, "Change. Wait. Face down."

I changed into my silk outfit and lay on the massage bed and waited for him to return.

The door opened and clicked shut. I didn't dare open my eyes. As soon as the hands made contact with my silken-clad body, I knew it wasn't my blue tracksuited man. The hands were too small and the perfume was far from manly. I eventually dared to open my eyes to find I was being massaged by a young woman with long, jet-black hair falling over her own silken-clad shoulders.

Her feminine attributes did not hinder her giving me one hour of painful torture. Not only did she use her hands but also her elbows, her knees and her feet. She pummelled me and yanked my limbs so strongly that I thought my joints were going to separate. During the whole of the hour not a word was spoken; the only sounds made were those of pain made by me, and they could hardly be described as words!

At the end of the hour the torture stopped and I heard the door click. I waited for a while and then got up, changed out of my silk outfit, dressed and exited the room. There was nobody about so I took the lift down to reception, scuttled across the floor and left. I couldn't cope with the thought of trying to explain to a taxi driver where I wanted to go, so walked back in the hope that walking would restore my body to normal.

I had survived!

19

—

HIMALAYAN TRUST UK

When I first decided I wanted to take a group of sixth-formers to the Himalayas, I searched for a company that would give me all the support I needed to ensure that the trek would be both safe and enjoyable. I travelled the country, visiting travel companies that provided such trips. It was difficult to decide.

During the 1991 October half term I was visiting my parents in Lincoln, so en route I decided to call in on a company called Classic Nepal based in Newton, Derbyshire. I did not hold out much hope. It seemed that they operated from their home and I doubted whether they had the contacts and the experience to fulfil my requirements.

Ann and Noel, who ran the company, were fantastic. Classic Nepal was a small company but they exuded confidence about their product, Nepal, without once putting me under any pressure. The year before, they had organised the Everest '53 Reunion Trek, with all those who had been on that expedition. If they were good enough for Ed Hillary, they were good enough for me.

Having gone into the meeting feeling it was going to be a waste of my time, I came out excited and motivated to make my dream come true. This was a big fillip, finding somebody I could work with, who would support me all the way and who would act as my safety net. It was the best two-hour meeting I have ever had and changed the course of my life.

As the concept of the King's Himalayan Club developed and I had two groups of students in training for expeditions to Everest in December '93 and Annapurna in April '94, I decided I needed a patron, a name I could put on a letterhead that would give me more credibility, particularly when seeking sponsorship. Ann and Noel suggested I get in touch with George Lowe, a veteran of the Everest '53 expedition. He also lived in Derbyshire.

Plucking up the courage, I wrote a letter to George asking him if he would be patron to King's Himalayan Club. He replied that he would be honoured to, but, in return, would I be a trustee of the Sir Edmund Hillary Himalayan Trust? That one letter also changed the course of my life. It never ceases to amaze me that a chance encounter, being in the right place at the right time, can determine which route your life takes.

So, I became a trustee of the Sir Edmund Hillary Himalayan Trust, which allowed me to have a charitable focus for each of my expeditions. It gave the students a reason to raise money for a particular project or initiative.

On that first Everest trip, we learnt that the Hillary Hospital at Khunde needed a microwave to thaw out IV fluids and other essential kit. We managed to raise the funds necessary to purchase these items but missionary zeal took control and we ended up with masses of donated medical items, all to be carried up to the hospital by porters. Of course, what works well in the UK may not be appropriate for a hospital almost 4000m high in the Himalayas. Much of what we had carried up had to be returned to Kathmandu, where it was more appropriate.

I was on a steep learning curve and enjoying every minute of it.

Often, in Kathmandu, people who wanted our support approached me. I, more often than not, found it difficult to say no. It's that missionary zeal again! As well as supporting the training of nurses for the trust, I found us supporting a Tashi Waldorf kindergarten run by a very inspirational Israeli, a home for disabled children and an orphanage.

As we moved away from Nepal for school expeditions we reduced what we did for the Himalayan Trust because we always found projects in the countries we were visiting. It was important that the students on the treks had projects with which they were directly involved. In India we focused on supporting schools, in Tanzania an orphanage, in Peru the school at Soqma, in Indonesia the building of public toilets on Komodo Island, to reduce the occurrence of dragon attacks when people squatted in the open, and in Kyrgyzstan we supported a home for disabled children and a home for abused women and children.

It was only when I retired from teaching in 2009 that I could give more of my attention to the trust, which by that time had changed to the Himalayan Trust UK.

In 2005, the then chairman, George Band, also of Everest '53, returned to the far east of Nepal, where Kangchenjunga lies, to celebrate the fiftieth anniversary of his first ascent. While there, the people of these remote mountains and valleys petitioned him to do for them what Ed Hillary had done for the Sherpas in the Khumbu. So began our work in the Taplejung District of Nepal. The name of the trust was changed to Himalayan Trust UK, as this area had no connection with Ed Hillary.

In 2007 a programme of teacher training and school development started in just one small, remote ward of Taplejung District, expanding in 2009 to cover a further four wards.

Having retired in August 2009, I decided I would visit the project area in October of that year. It was a long and complicated journey then to get up to Taplejung. It still is, but it was more so then.

Taking one guide with me, an ex-pupil of Sapta Gandaki School in Kathmandu, which the Himalayan Club had supported over many years, I took a flight from Kathmandu to Bhadrapur, in the south-east corner of Nepal, very close to the border with India. From there, we took a car to take us on the long journey up to Phidim.

The car was a very lightweight Suzuki Maruti. After an hour or so, we reached the beginning of the long climb round hairpin bend after hairpin bend.

After about four hours we reached the town of Ilam, the tea-growing centre of east Nepal. The climb continued over one ridge, then steeply down to the valley floor before another long climb. I was sitting in the back of the vehicle and with every hairpin bend was swinging from one side of the vehicle to the other, sliding on the mock leather seat, as I did not have the benefit or security of a seatbelt.

All of a sudden, on one of the bends we met a jeep, much better suited to the road than we were, coming down a little too fast. He failed to get round and gave us a mighty whack in the side.

Suddenly, in the middle of nowhere, we had a crowd gathering around the two vehicles. Everybody had an opinion and they all wanted it heard. I got out of the vehicle and sat on the roadside, bemused by the scene that was unfolding in front of me. The gist of it was that the driver of the jeep was to blame and it was he who had to pay compensation to my driver. How much? The answer to that question seemed to be what most of the arguing was about, and it was a heated one.

People came and went and came back again. Eventually, the jeep driver's father came and a semblance of order seemed to come with him. A sum was agreed and the money changed hands. This had taken three hours. The light was beginning to fade and we still had some distance to go to get to Phidim.

We limped all the way to Phidim. It was late. I was hungry, tired and fed up with being lurched around every one of the hundreds of bends in the road. We found a hotel to stay in. The term "hotel" I use loosely. I had a bed. I chose to use my sleeping bag in favour of unwashed, flea-infested blankets. In the night I could hear rats scrabbling around my room and when I wanted to pop to the loo in the night I found a massive dog lying against my door. I didn't know whether it was friendly or otherwise.

After a fairly restless night, I began to assess the situation and look at options. Clearly, the vehicle we had travelled in so far was in no fit state to continue. The road from Phidim to Taplejung was not tarmacked but was a deeply rutted mud track. The journey would take at least twelve hours. The state of the road dictated that I would have to hire a four-wheel drive jeep or Land Cruiser, which proved to be beyond my budget. I could take the local bus. There wasn't one for another four days! Could I bear being in a room with rats and a massive guard dog for that length of time? No. Also, that would take a huge amount of time out of my itinerary; once I reached Taplejung, it would take me a further three days to walk to the nearest school. By then I would have to turn round and travel back. It was not worth it.

To the surprise of my guide, I decided my only option was to go back to Kathmandu, which is what I did. There was plenty there to occupy me at the orphanage I still supported and at Sapta Gandaki School until my flight home.

Although this trip was a failure in many ways, it taught me that nothing is ever easy in Nepal. What I had encountered on my journey is what the Nepalese encounter daily. They accept that this is the situation and they live with it. Despite all my travels to Nepal, I still had not developed that inner karma, that "what will be, will be" approach to life.

Soon afterwards I became the head of the education programme for the trust and later, again, the role of deputy chairman.

In 2015, under these two titles, I decided it was time for me to visit the schools in our project area. The road from Phidim to Taplejung had now been sealed, making the journey considerably quicker.

I was travelling on my own again. I was actually quite nervous. I was so used to travelling with a group, constantly focused on their welfare and enjoyment, making sure that they were physically and mentally well. Sometimes, when I have been slightly under the weather, the fact that I am responsible for them makes me forget my own woes. Who am I going to look after on this trip? Who is going to make sure I am feeling well and happy and whom can I rely on to help me if I need help?

Three days before my arrival in Taplejung, a gas cylinder in a hotel exploded in the early evening and the resulting fire quickly spread from the hotel to the tightly packed houses, shops and businesses around it. Most of the buildings were built of stone but had timber framed roofs with corrugated iron sheets on top. All the internal walls were of wood, very dry wood, which quickly caught fire and helped it spread very quickly. There are no fire services in Taplejung, the nearest being in Ilam, at least five hours away, so the people, having escaped from their burning properties, could do little but watch as their homes and possessions disappeared in front of them. The metal pylons carrying cables along the street melted in the heat.

The only way the authorities could hope to contain the fire and prevent it spreading through the old market streets was to bulldoze some properties in an effort to create a firebreak. The combination of this action and the arrival of the fire tenders the following day finally contained the fire, brought it under control and extinguished it.

The fire had destroyed forty-five houses, shops and businesses and displaced 132 families who had lost everything. The estimated cost of the damage was NRs300 million (US$3 million)

By the time I arrived, smoke was still rising from the rubble. It was a scene of absolute desolation, with people picking through the burnt remains for anything they could find that might have survived the conflagration. One woman simply stood in the remains of her house, staring at the space the fire had left, not just at the vacuum around her but in her mind also.

There was an eerie silence about the scene, a reverence to those numbed by the disaster by those passing by, who knew that this could have happened anywhere in town, that it could so easily have happened to them.

I talked with some of the victims, and thankfully nobody was hurt, but they were feeling emotional pain, only deepened by the apparent lack of support from the government. An emergency fund had been set up by the district administration office, but until funds became available there was little the authorities could do with their own limited capabilities. A token gesture had been made and some emergency funding had been handed out; people had been provided with sheltered accommodation or had found themselves with other family members. Local businesspeople were rallying round, providing food and clothing to help ease the pain.

One of the most poignant images was of a family digging deep into the rubble to retrieve their rice stocks. Remarkably, some of the sacks were intact, protected from the fire by the collapsed stone walls. I watched them picking out the burnt bits in the hope that their rice would still be edible.

Another was of a wooden shack that had once been a shoe shop but had now been bulldozed out of the way to prevent the fire spreading. Thankfully it had worked, but the sight of the shopkeeper trying to retrieve her shoes from the debris, her only source of income, was a distressing image of desperation, anger, frustration and acceptance.

I visited the district administration officer to ask what sort of support he was able to give the community affected by the fire. Not a lot, it seemed, as it was going to have to rely upon the building up of the emergency fund. I had already been in touch with my fellow trustees, and was able to donate US$10,000, giving the fund a much-needed boost.

I needn't have worried about how I was going to cope on my own. I wasn't on my own. I had Rajendra with me. Rajendra is the district coordinator for our partner NGO, REED Nepal. He spends much of his time out in the field supporting schools through teacher training, resource management and development and ensuring that schools provide a child-friendly environment. He was my guide as well as arranging all my visits. It was a fascinating trip and I enjoyed every minute of my time in many of the project schools.

As enjoyable as it was, it was exhausting. These schools are remote and so far flung, up precipitous slopes to be ascended each day. Playgrounds were perched on these slopes and I could not help thinking how far they would have to go to retrieve a ball.

Once at the school, I would have to compose myself so that I could observe classes and engage in discussions with the heads, teachers, school management committees and the wider community. Wherever I went, the community came to see me.

The conversations were taxing in themselves. Often, when I asked a question through Rajendra, he would have to translate it into Nepali. Some of the participants might not speak Nepali as their first language, so it would have to be translated into Limbu, the local dialect. Answers would come back to me by the same circuitous route, ensuring that these discussions took some considerable time.

Continuous assessment of the needs of each school was on my agenda. I always had to be mindful not to promise anything, however strongly I agreed with the need. The Himalayan Trust has a core commitment to teacher training and that is sacrosanct. Only when that is guaranteed can the Trust begin to look at the extras that enhance a school's environment or performance.

Normally, when I am out in the field I am strictly vegetarian. Opportunities for meat are few and far between. Anyway, I always want to err on the side of caution. Meat and poor hygiene can result in upset tummies.

I was visiting Deurali School, which serves a subsistence agricultural community. The school is perched on a terrace 750m above the valley floor. I learnt that I was the first white face to visit the village for five years. Hence there was a celebrity status attached to my visit.

To mark the occasion, the village wanted to "kill the fatted calf" and provide me with a feast. As there was no accommodation available, I was camping on the earthen school playground. All the children had gone home. I was sitting in my tent, writing up my notes from the day, when, eventually, I was invited up to a house perched on a nearby terrace. There were one or two village elders there for the occasion.

The fatted calf turned out to be a skinny chicken. Normally I would say that a piece of tender chicken would be a welcome addition to the tedium of dal bhat, which I was eating meal after meal. In Nepal they don't take the breast off and separate the thighs and drumsticks; they hack at the bird with a cleaver and put everything into the pot. In among the scraps of meat there are splinters of bone, the chicken's comb and, worst of all, clawed feet. I did the best I could, not wishing to offend them for their kindness, but it was really quite inedible.

After the meal I was escorted to my tent along narrow paths around terraces. As I settled for the night, two dogs joined me on the playground and started barking. "What is this strange green object on our playground? We'll bark at it all night." That is what they did. They positioned themselves, one either side of the tent, barking in stereo.

It was a disturbed night.

At 4.00am the cockerels started their morning call. As soon as one started, they all started and, as there was one on the terrace just below my tent, there was no escape. At least the dogs had gone.

By now I was beginning to feel a little uncomfortable in the bowel region. The skinny chicken was threatening to take its revenge out on me.

At 5.00am the human dawn chorus joined the cockerels with a clearing of the nasal passages followed by a hearty spit. My stomach turned. I did manage to doze off as the cockerels abated and the spitting silenced, delaying the inevitable visit to the toilet.

At 6.00am I became aware of whispered voices outside my tent. About a dozen children, many of whom had never seen a white face before, or could not remember seeing one, had gathered outside my tent waiting for me to get up. The way my stomach was feeling, they were going to be in for a surprise.

I could hold it no longer. I threw on some clothes, unzipped my tent to a sea of smiling faces, the children squatting in an arc around my tent. They watched me closely as I emerged clutching a toilet roll.

They followed me to the toilet at the end of the playground. As I shut the door, they squatted again.

As I, too, squatted I could watch them through cracks in the door. No one likes an audience at these times. Unfortunately, these were not the best of times, and as much as I tried, I could not perform in silence. As the chicken from the night before escaped, the children giggled at my performance. They had the decency to try and suppress their giggles but I was watching them. Had I not felt so dreadful I would have laughed with them.

Eventually, I emerged from the toilet and returned to my tent, much relieved. The children followed me and assumed their encircling positions. Five minutes later they followed me back to the toilet!

I spent five weeks in Nepal, wandering the hills, visiting schools in remote communities. It proved to be one of the most rewarding trips I had done. I got to know a little about the lives of these people and the difficulties they face. Why have some of these schools not got access to fresh water? Why are some teachers not paid a proper wage, simply because they are not part of the government allocation? Some communities, eager for their children to receive an education, collectively fund those teachers. There are so many problems, many of which could be solved with relatively small amounts of money but are beyond the means of the Himalayan Trust or are not part of their remit.

With so many things to think about and the level of concentration needed whenever there were discussions, I felt I needed a second pair of ears and eyes, somebody to share ideas and the responsibility of the role of trustee, in charge of education. Who did I know that would fit the bill and bring a great deal of expertise and enthusiasm to the role? I knew exactly who I wanted.

I returned home inspired and motivated to do more to support these wonderful people. That motivation was put to the test three days after I returned. On 25 April 2015, Nepal was rocked by a devastating earthquake that killed almost 9000 and injured nearly 22,000 people. Nepal was on its knees. Part of me wished I had still been there, out in the hills helping. I was more use at home. I put out an appeal to King's School, whose pupils had benefited from so many Nepalese experiences, and the wider community of Worcestershire. Within days, I had amassed eight tons of tents, sleeping bags and blankets.

Using a friend's barn, we packed everything on pallets ready to be airlifted to Nepal. Using contacts, we managed to get a road haulier to transport it all to Heathrow, where an airline was prepared to fly it to Nepal, as part of their contribution to the mercy mission.

The damage had been extensive, the more so when a second earthquake struck on 12 May, causing significantly more damage.

When you donate something, it is reassuring to know that it has reached its target. A few weeks after the shipment had gone to Nepal, I was giving a fundraising presentation, showing pictures of the earthquake and its aftermath, when one of the assembled audience recognised his daughter's sleeping bag being handed out to a child.

A number of the schools I had visited, including Deurali, were seriously damaged. It was a blessing that the first, most damaging earthquake occurred on a Saturday when schools were closed. Had it been any other day of the week, the number of deaths and injuries would have been much higher, if stone walled classrooms had collapsed on classrooms full of children.

In the weeks following the earthquakes the Himalayan Trust raised hundreds of thousands of pounds and embarked of a "Build Back Better" programme in partnership with the New Zealand Himalayan Trust and the Australian Himalayan Foundation, both of which had very strong links with Ed Hillary.

First, we wanted to bring a little normality into the lives of children, to get functioning those schools most seriously damaged. We built TLCs (temporary learning centres), which would allow lessons to continue while schools were rebuilt.

Using a proven earthquake-resistant design, the three collaborative organisations rebuilt 165 classrooms in the Everest and Kangchenjunga regions.

I returned to Nepal in 2016 to monitor the rebuilding of our schools and to reassure the schools and communities that the Himalayan Trust UK was working hard to support them. I was not alone. I had approached a former headmaster of King's School Worcester, Tim Keyes, who had recently retired. Tim had been on the millennium expedition to King's Peak (Nobby's View) as a member of staff. More importantly, I had total respect for him as a headmaster, and as a friend, and knew that he would bring so much knowledge, skill and understanding to the role of trustee.

Tim and I made subsequent visits in 2018 and 2019, working in partnership with the trust's health team, who were also rolling out a programme of health provision improvements. He proved to be a valued trustee, fulfilling his role as additional eyes and ears and decision maker.

Much of my time is now taken with promoting the work of the trust, securing the extra funding that is needed to ensure that schools are able to provide a quality education to children. Hopefully, the opportunities we provide will allow them to climb above the poverty line and to seek worthwhile and rewarding futures.

Thankfully, because of the support from a group of trekking friends, all schools now have access to fresh water.

One issue I was particularly determined to solve was the problem that children face with hunger during the school day. As you know, from my experiences in Deurali, children get up very early. Before they go to school they will fulfil a number of family chores, feeding livestock, fetching water etc. At some point they will eat breakfast.

School starts at 10.00am. Many children will endure a one- to two-hour walk to school, up and down hill, on rough tracks. There are no provisions to give the children a lunch during the school day. By the time school finishes at 4.00pm they have another long walk to get home before they can have any food. It is too long for growing children to go without food. Their concentration levels drop as the day wears on, reducing their ability to learn.

The Himalayan Trust now works in thirty-five schools. It would be financially impossible and wrong for us to build a cooking facility in each school and maintain a fund to ensure that there was food each day. There had to be a simpler solution. There was. Thermos lunchboxes.

If I were able to raise the funds to allow every child to own a Thermos lunchbox, it would then be the responsibility of the school to educate the parents to put food into them each day. We ran a pilot scheme with 600 children and the outcome was remarkable. The parental provision of rice and vegetables each day allowed the children to concentrate on all their lessons, not just those in the morning. School attendance improved because children no longer felt the need to abscond in the afternoons. The proof of the pudding was that, after a period of a few months, the schools registered improved learning outcomes for every child in the pilot scheme.

In 2019 I visited one of the schools taking part in the pilot scheme and it was a joy to watch as the children washed their hands before queuing up to receive their lunch, sitting in a group on the playground, tucking in and enjoying their food. When they had finished, they rinsed out their boxes and put them on the wall to dry in the sun. At the end of the day, they would take them home, ready for the next day.

This was the evidence I needed to encourage people to buy into the project, to supply the funds needed for every child to have a Thermos lunchbox. As the children have returned to school following the pandemic, they have received a Thermos lunchbox from the Himalayan Trust UK.

Of course, there are always obstacles cropping up to hinder our work or divert our attention. The recent pandemic closed schools in Nepal for six months, casting fear and anxiety in the young minds of the children. In the middle of the pandemic a landslide wiped out half of a school, something that could happen at any time to many of the schools we work with. These challenges have to be faced and dealt with, not ignored.

In 2020 I had to cancel two trips to the schools, but, rest assured, I shall be out there as soon as circumstances allow.

ACKNOWLEDGEMENTS

None of what you have read in the preceding pages would have been possible if it had not been for the support I was shown along the way, from those first tentative steps in 1993 to almost one hundred expeditions and trips now in my portfolio. This is my opportunity to thank them.

Ann Brooks and Noel Walsh, of Classic Nepal, later changed to Classic Journeys, were exceptional in preparing me for the adventures I was dreaming up. I was on a steep learning curve and I doubt I would have survived without them.

When I first proposed the idea of taking a group of sixth-formers to Nepal, the headmaster of the time gave me the thumbs-up but dampened his permission with, "Don't come running to me when it goes wrong!" Hardly encouraging words, but his deputy, Tim Hickson, was far more encouraging and has been a loyal supporter ever since. He saw the benefit pupils would receive, not from the expedition alone but from the training experience that led up to the expedition, and knew that, in a competitive world, such an experience could, possibly, give them a slight advantage.

I could not have done any of the student trips if I had not had the willingness of staff to give up a large part of their holiday time to help train, and then to accompany me on the trips. It was a huge sacrifice for some, who deserted their families for a month, at a time when family time was precious. With some, it was not just once but several times, and I shall be eternally grateful to them.

I want to make particular mention of Tim Keyes, who became headmaster of King's a few years into the Himalayan Expeditions. If he had had any reservations about what I was doing, he could have stopped it immediately. He didn't, or, if he did, he kept them to himself. He saw the value it was providing the students and it gave us an edge over our closest rivals in a very competitive market. I decided the best way to have the head on side was to get him involved on a trip, and it was a joy to have him join me in 2000 on the King's Peak/Nobby's View trek. I think there were one or two occasions when he thought he was going to die, but he never lost his faith in me. I am so pleased that he and I can now work together on the education programme of the Himalayan Trust UK.

Similarly, part of my safety net was to assure the parents that we had professional medics to ensure the wellbeing and health of their children. Many of the doctors had to give up their own holiday allowances, or paid for a locum to cover their absence. They acted beyond the call of duty and gave me, the school and the parents peace of mind, in the knowledge that everything was being done to keep everybody safe.

I would like to thank the students, and there are over a thousand of them, who jumped at the opportunities I provided for them. Their enthusiasm knew no bounds. That, in turn, fed my own enthusiasm and drove me to find trips that were unique to each group, that no other student group from King's had done, so their memories were theirs and theirs alone.

When parents send their children on school trips they expect the level of care to keep their children safe. I know, looking back at some of the stories I have included, we had some fairly high-risk moments. I am extremely relieved that I never had to have a very awkward conversation with parents as to why their child did not come home. Sadly, it happens on some school trips. I am grateful for the support the parent body gave me in allowing me to take their children on a memorable and often life-changing experience.

In all of the countries we visited we were extremely well looked after by agents, guides, Sherpas, crew and porters. Without their expert local knowledge none of what we have achieved would have been possible. Their input opened so many doors for us, so that we got closer to the local communities we came into contact with, learnt about their – often – very hard lives, providing us with a new perspective of the world in which we live.

The Himalayan Trust UK has been a huge part of my life for the last twenty-five years. It has given me a focus to channel my energies into to provide my groups, particularly in the early days, with a charitable objective to work towards. The trustees have always been supportive in my desire to get things done. I particularly want to highlight the impact that George and Mary Lowe had in encouraging me to explore the world and to share it with my students. Sadly, George is no longer with us, but I think he knew how grateful I was for his patronage when I was getting the Himalayan Club off the ground.

The King's School parents, not satisfied with entrusting their children to me, decided that they too wanted to see the world, insisting that I take them on trips, not with their children but without them. These proved successful and I am grateful that they trusted me to give them very special experiences, even if some of them were quite challenging. There are many who come with me again and again, creating some strong friendships along the way.

I want to thank everybody who has been involved in any capacity and supported the charitable fundraising, either for the Himalayan Trust or for any of the many projects in the countries we have visited around the world. The projects have been numerous. Some have been more successful than others. None of them could have achieved anything without the financial support and fundraising that has occurred over the years. We have generated well over £300,000 to support remote, marginalised and needy communities in Asia, Africa and South America.

I want to thank my family. I apologise to my children for all the times I was away when they might have needed me. It heartens me to see them now making their own marks on the world. My daughter, who at fifteen years old, while climbing Skiddaw, shouted, "I hate you, Dad! I never want to go walking with you again!" can now be seen walking dogs on the Malvern Hills twice a day. That's my girl! She finally came to Nepal with me in 2019. I wanted her to see some of the things that I am passionate about. She now understands.

Stephen came to Nepal with me in 2002, to India in 2006 and again to Nepal in 2013. That last time we were heading up to Everest. At 4000m I started to cough up blood and decided that I should descend. I asked Stephen if he would lead the group for me. He stepped into my shoes and not only filled them but owned them. He has adventure in his heart and he makes me extremely proud.

Finally, I want to thank Angela. I know I have dedicated this book to her, but I am nothing without her. She has supported me all the way, and 100% of the time. She even married me, knowing that there were going to be significant chunks of each year when, if she didn't come with me, she would be left "home alone".

When we both left King's in 2009, we were given an incredible send-off at Junior King's Day, the end-of-year prizegiving day. Richard Bellfield, the head of the junior school, talked at length about me. When he turned his attention to Angela, he said, "And then there is the voice of reason…" Occasionally, Angela has to bring me back to earth, to reboot me, to be the voice of reason. I cannot thank her enough. Thank you, Angela, for being there all the time. Oh, and by the way, there was an extra foot of snow on the summit of Stok Kangri when I climbed it!